piano
vocal
guitar

Frank Sinatra
romance
songs from the heart

T0101558

ISBN-13: 978-1-4234-3136-7
ISBN-10: 1-4234-3136-7

HAL•LEONARD®
CORPORATION

7777 W. BLUEMOUND RD. P.O. BOX 13819 MILWAUKEE, WI 53213

Visit Hal Leonard Online at
www.halleonard.com

CONTENTS

I'VE GOT YOU UNDER MY SKIN

from BORN TO DANCE

Words and Music by
COLE PORTER

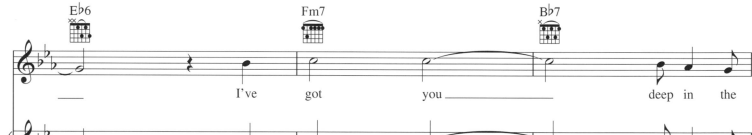

I've got you _____ un-der my skin, _____

I've got you _____ deep in the

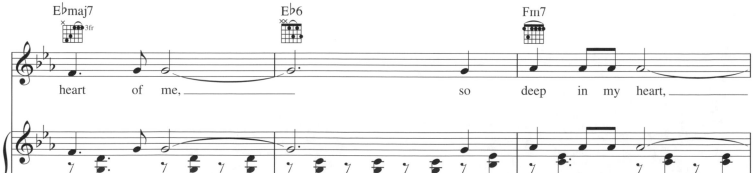

heart of me, _____ so deep in my heart, _____

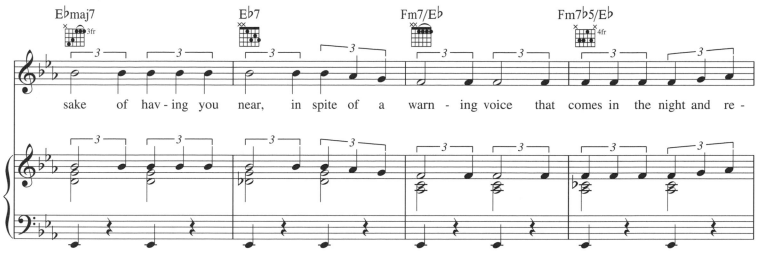

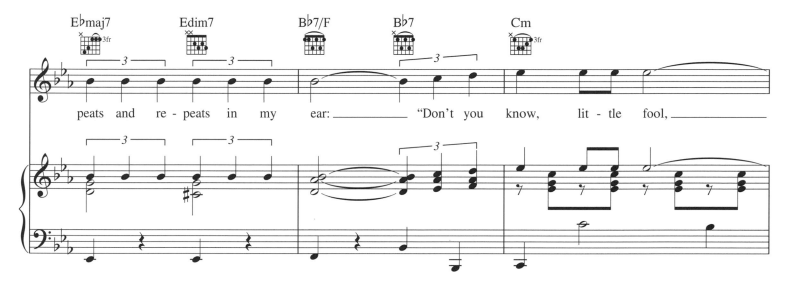

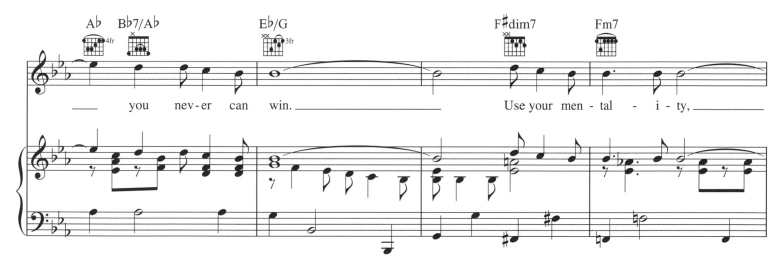

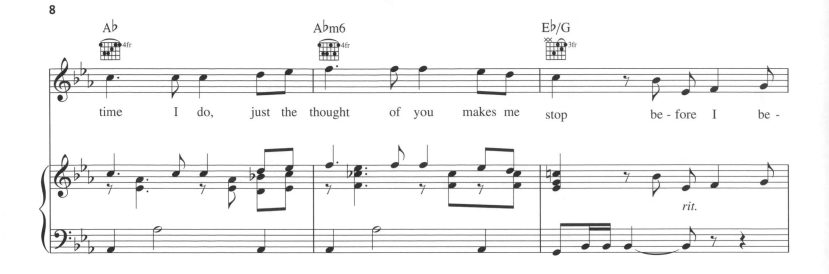

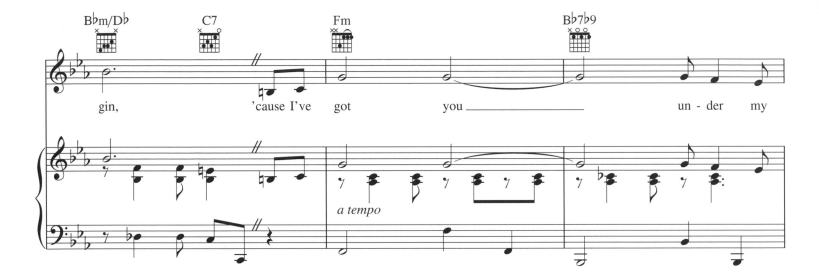

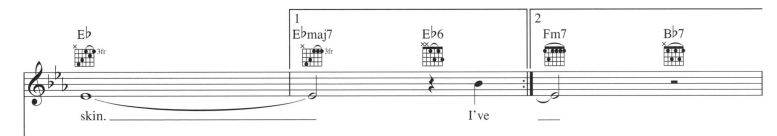

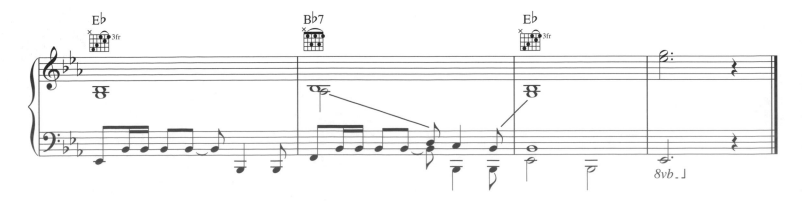

TIME AFTER TIME

from the Metro-Goldwyn-Mayer Picture IT HAPPENED IN BROOKLYN

Words by SAMMY CAHN
Music by JULE STYNE

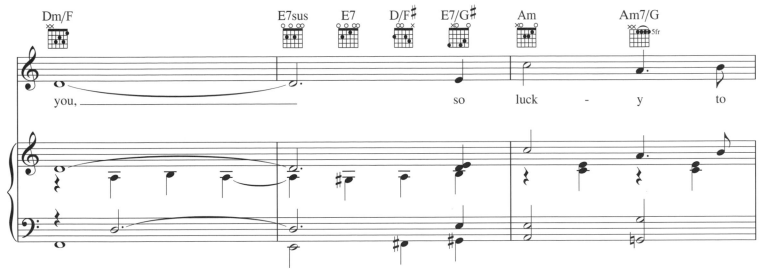

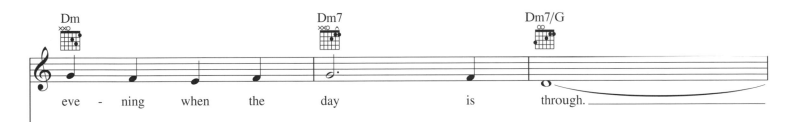

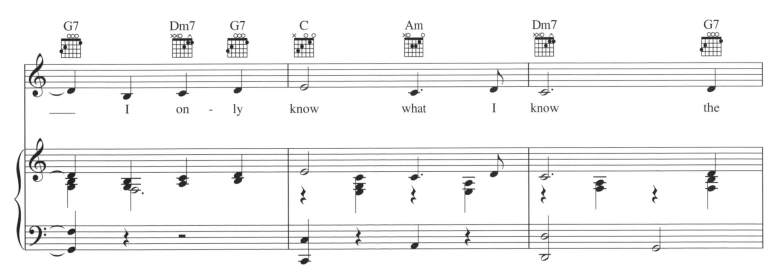

12

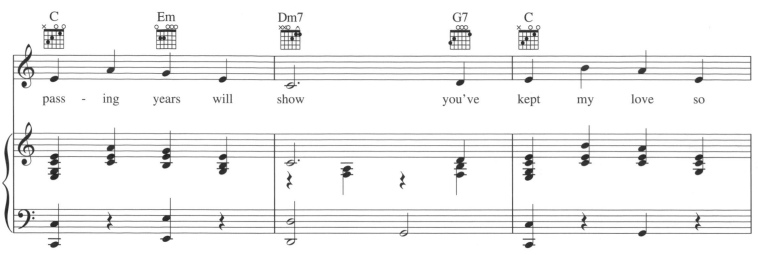

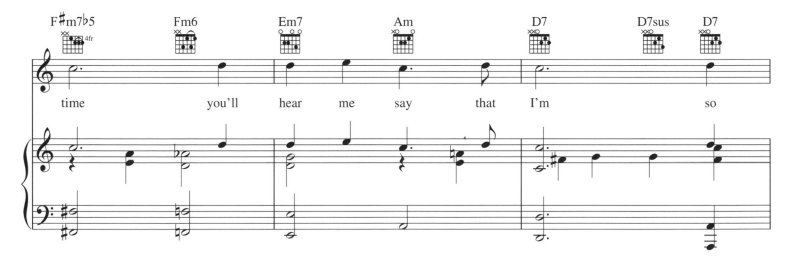

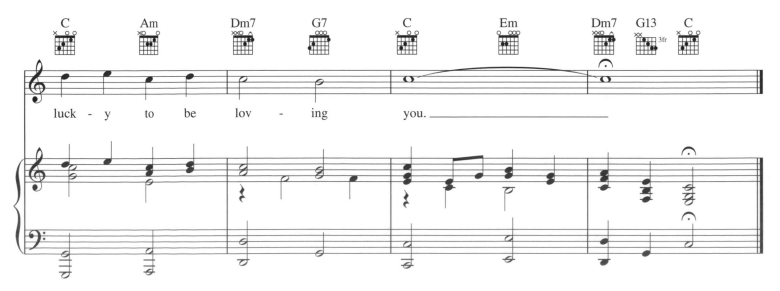

DAY BY DAY
Theme from the Paramount Television Series DAY BY DAY

Words and Music by SAMMY CAHN,
AXEL STORDAHL and PAUL WESTON

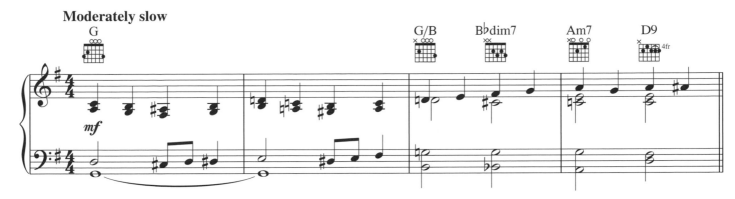

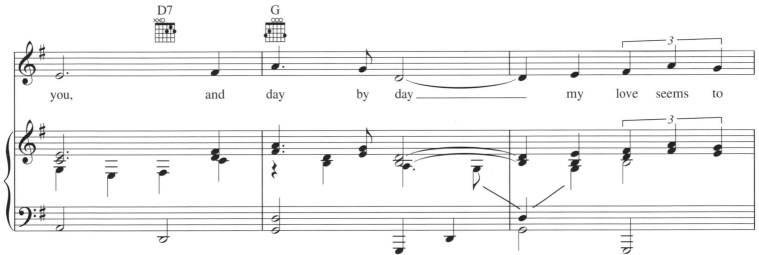

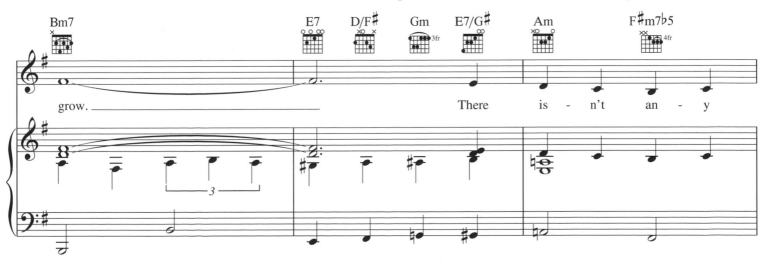

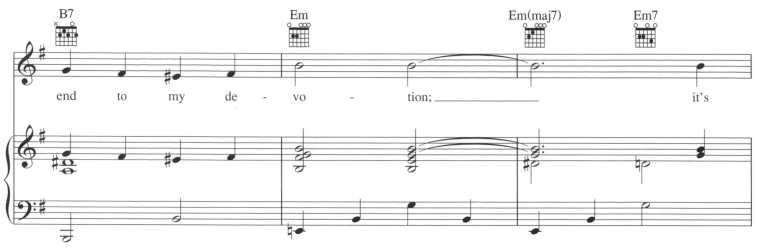

end to my de - vo - tion; _____ it's

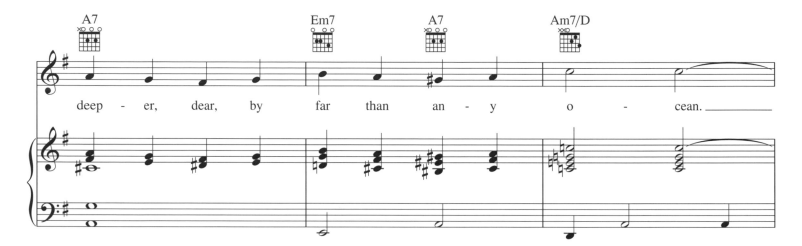

deep - er, dear, by far than an - y o - cean. _____

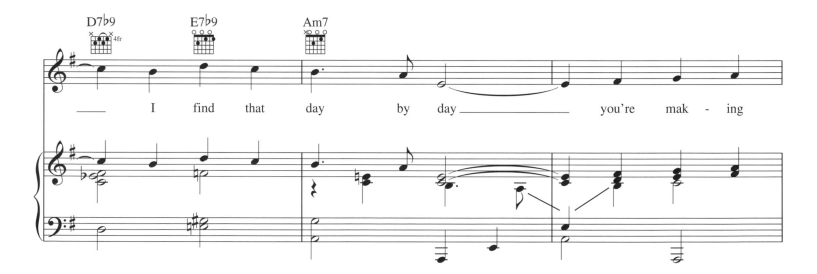

_____ I find that day by day _____ you're mak - ing

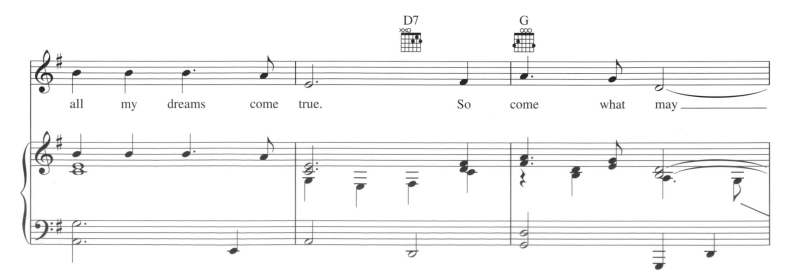

all my dreams come true. So come what may _____

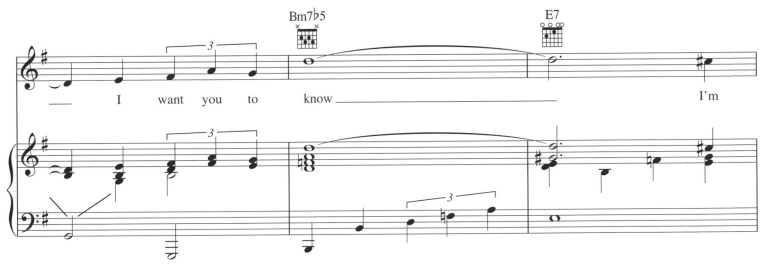

I want you to know _____ I'm

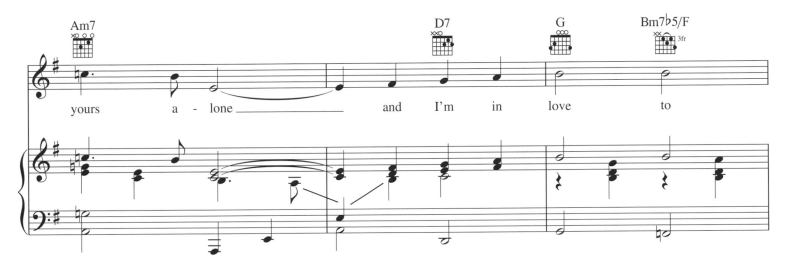

yours a - lone _____ and I'm in love to

stay, as we go through the years, day by

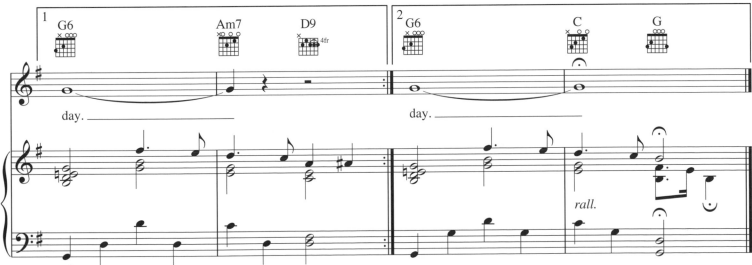

day. _____ day. _____

ALL THE WAY
from THE JOKER IS WILD

Words by SAMMY CAHN
Music by JAMES VAN HEUSEN

When some-bod-y loves you, it's no good un-less he loves you all the way.
When some-bod-y needs you, it's no good un-less she needs you all the way.

Hap-py to be near you, when you need some-one to cheer you all the way.
Thru the good or lean years and for all the in-be-tween years, come what may.

Tall-er than the tall-est tree is,
Who knows where the road will lead us,

TOO MARVELOUS FOR WORDS

Words by JOHNNY MERCER
Music by RICHARD A. WHITING

20

you. To be eu-phe-mis-ti-cal, to be eu-lo-gis-ti-cal, I

have to come up with a mil-lion words that no one ev-er knew. I try to be

log-i-cal and sen-si-ble, but I'm in-com-pre-hen-si-ble when-

ev-er I be-gin to find a phrase for

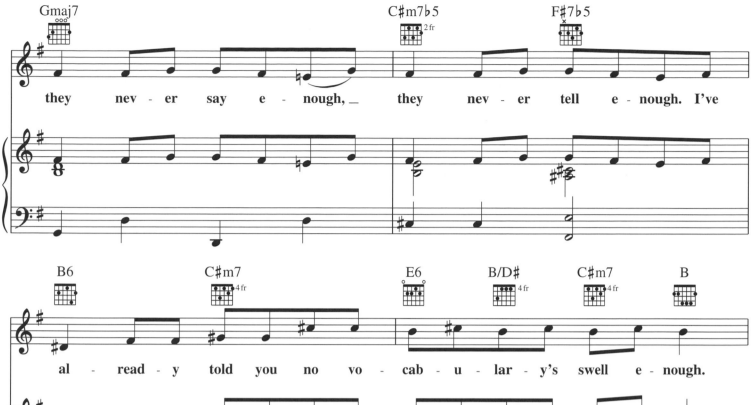

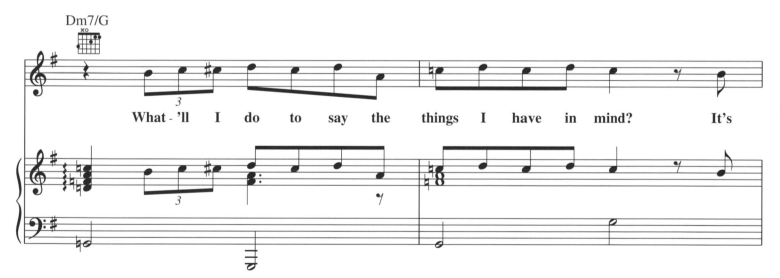

MY FUNNY VALENTINE
from BABES IN ARMS

Words by LORENZ HART
Music by RICHARD RODGERS

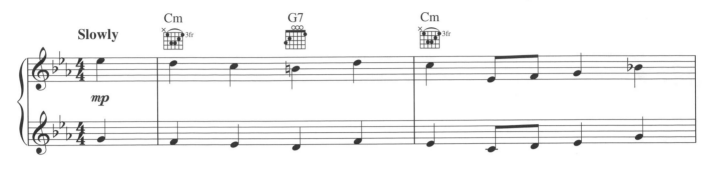

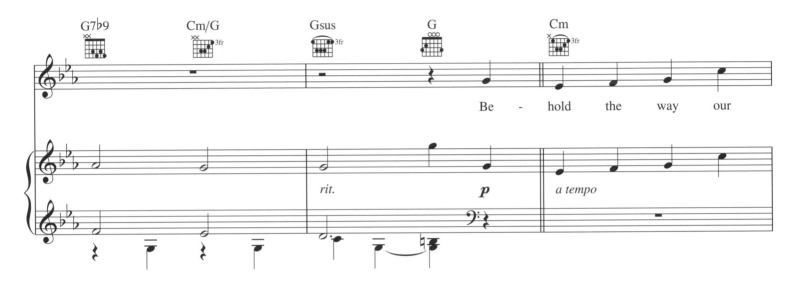

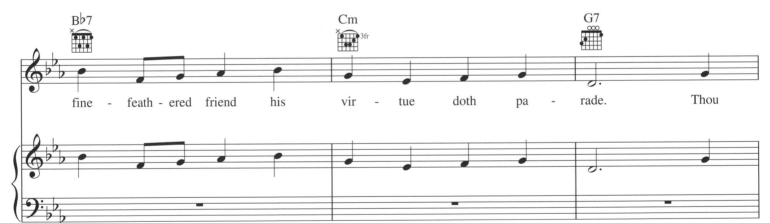

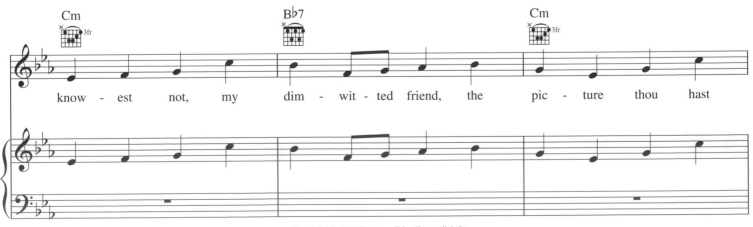

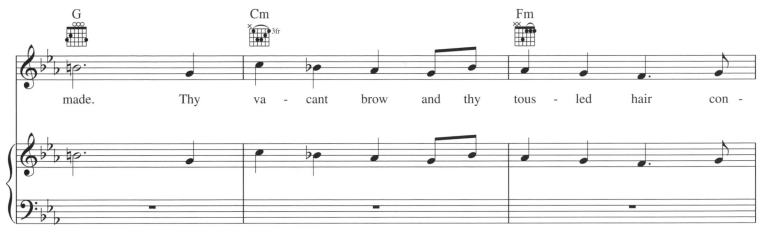

made. Thy va - cant brow and thy tous - led hair con-

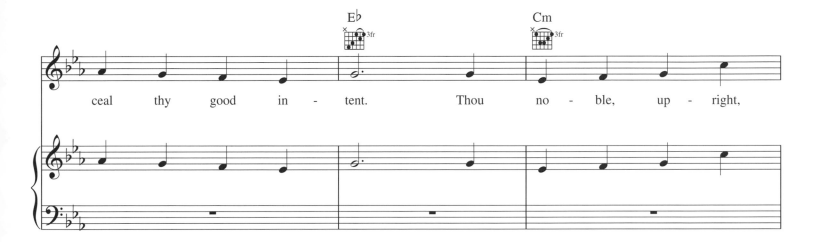

ceal thy good in - tent. Thou no - ble, up - right,

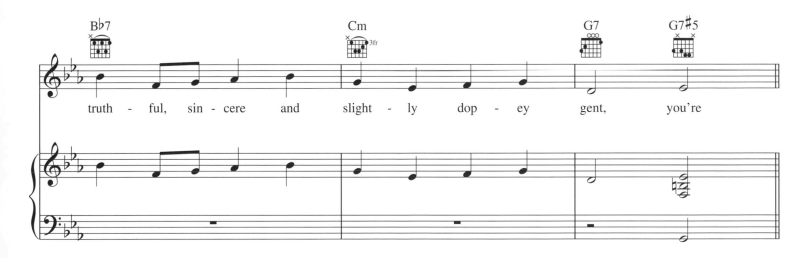

truth - ful, sin - cere and slight - ly dop - ey gent, you're

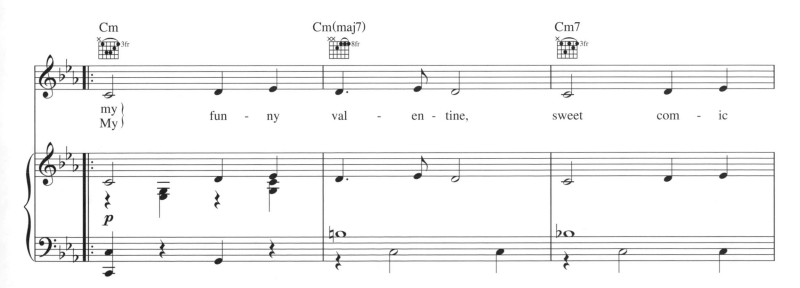

my }
My } fun - ny val - en - tine, sweet com - ic

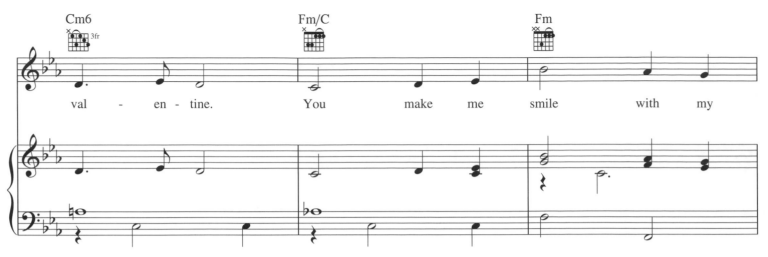

val - en - tine. You make me smile with my

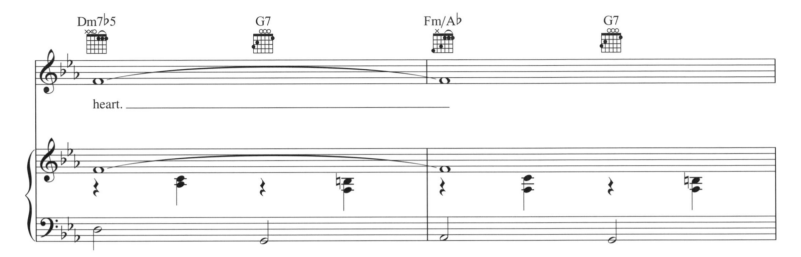

heart. _____

Your looks are laugh - a - ble, un - pho - to -

graph - a - ble, yet you're my fav - 'rite work of

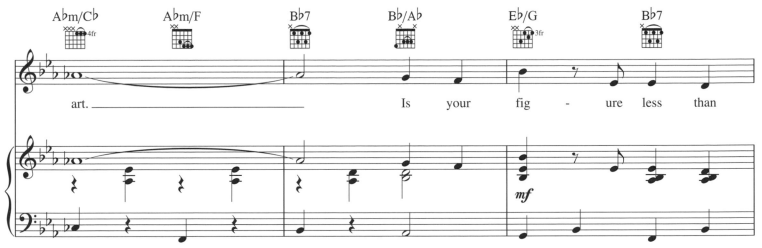

art. _____ Is your fig - ure less than

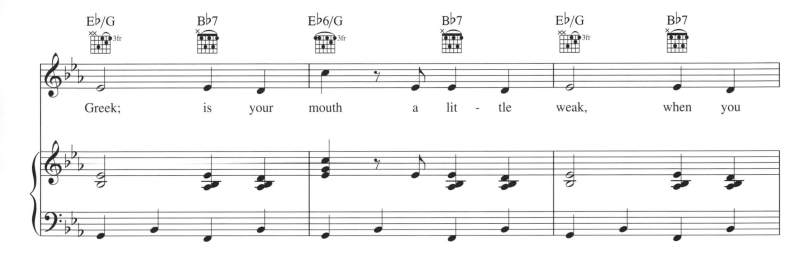

Greek; is your mouth a lit - tle weak, when you

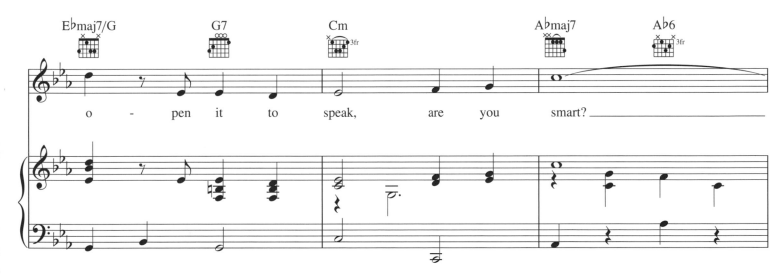

o - pen it to speak, are you smart? _____

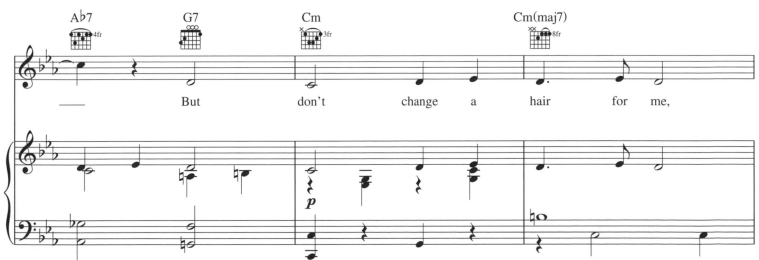

_____ But don't change a hair for me,

30

LOVE IS HERE TO STAY

from GOLDWYN FOLLIES
from AN AMERICAN IN PARIS

Music and Lyrics by GEORGE GERSHWIN
and IRA GERSHWIN

With motion

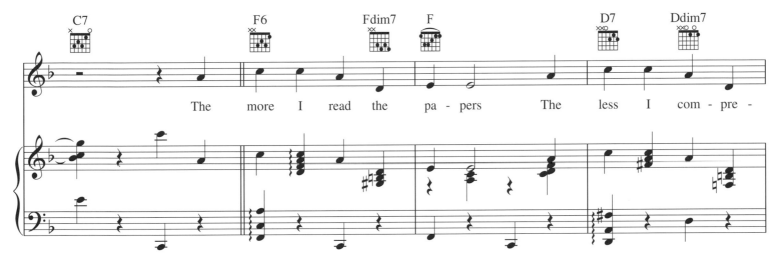

The more I read the pa-pers The less I com-pre-

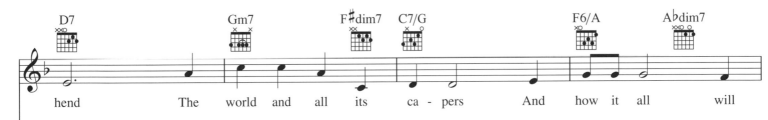

hend The world and all its ca-pers And how it all will

end. Noth-ing seems to be last-ing, But

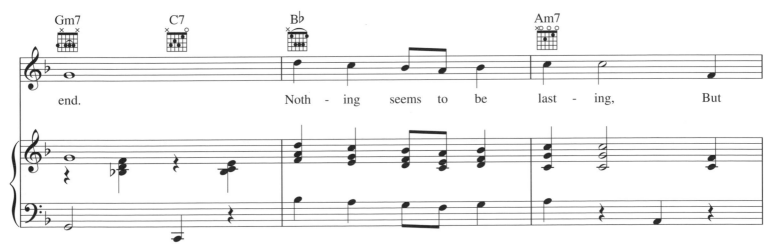

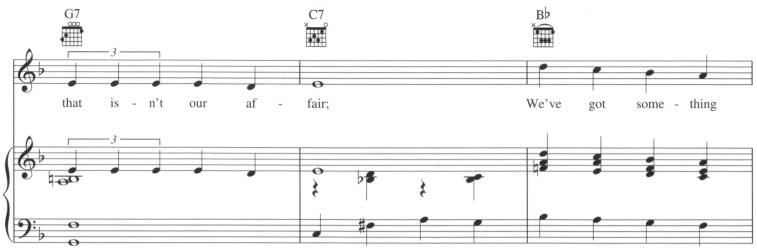

that is - n't our af - fair; We've got some - thing

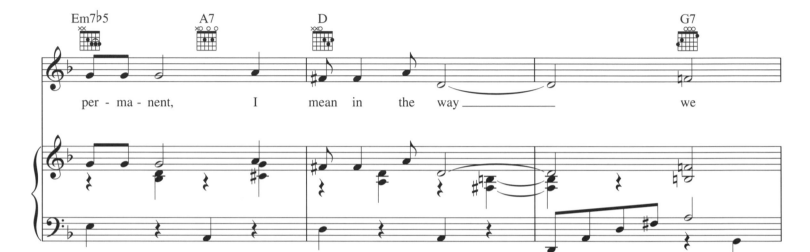

per - ma - nent, I mean in the way _____ we

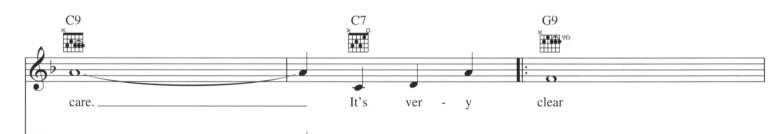

care. _____ It's ver - y clear

Our love is here to stay;

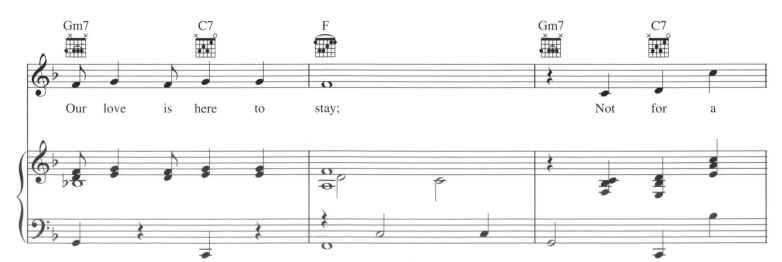

Not for a

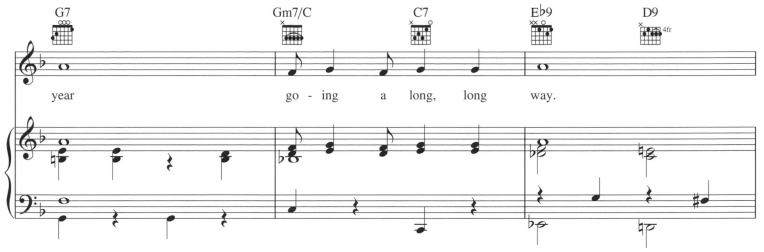

year   go - ing a long, long way.

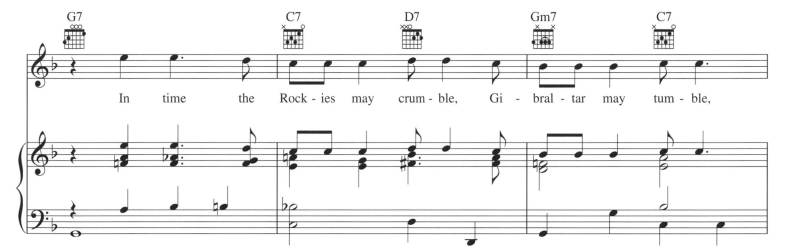

In time the Rock - ies may crum - ble, Gi - bral - tar may tum - ble,

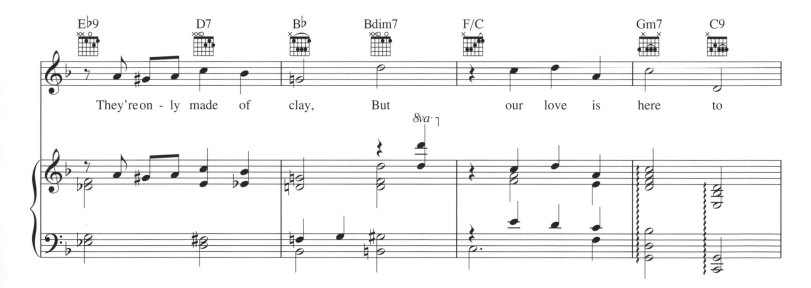

They're on - ly made of clay, But   our love is here to

stay. _____ It's ver - y   stay. _____

I'VE GOT A CRUSH ON YOU

Music and Lyrics by GEORGE GERSHWIN
and IRA GERSHWIN

Lightly, playfully

He: How
She: How

glad the man - y mil - lions of An - na - belles and Lil - lians would be ____
glad a mil - lion lad - dies from mil - lion - aires to cad - dies would be ____

____ to cap - ture me! _____ But you had such per - sist - ence, you

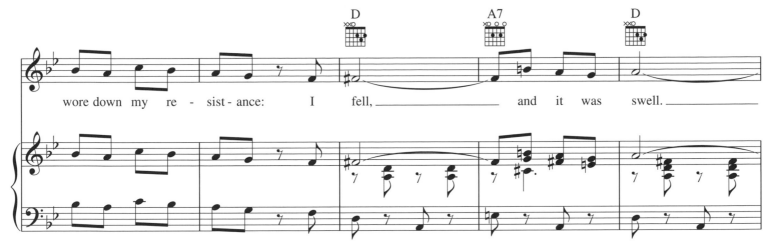

wore down my re - sist - ance: I fell, _____ and it was swell. _____

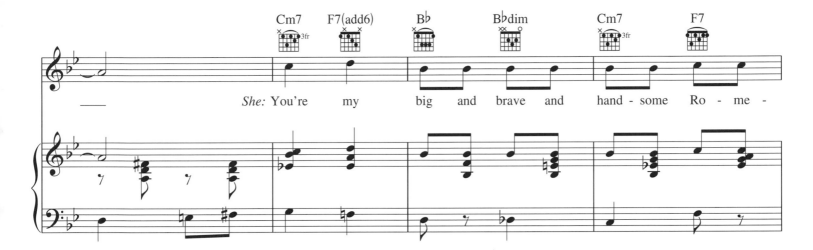

___ *She:* You're my big and brave and hand - some Ro - me -

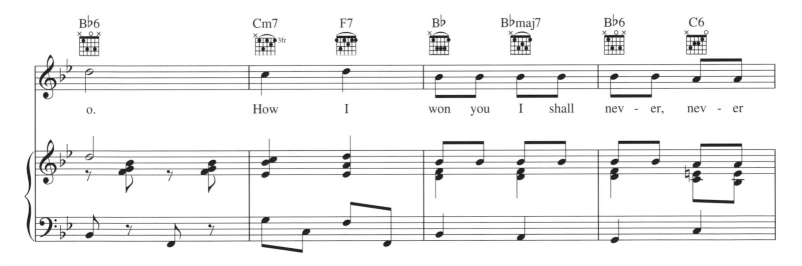

o. How I won you I shall nev - er, nev - er

know. *He:* It's not that you're at - trac - tive, but, oh, my heart grew

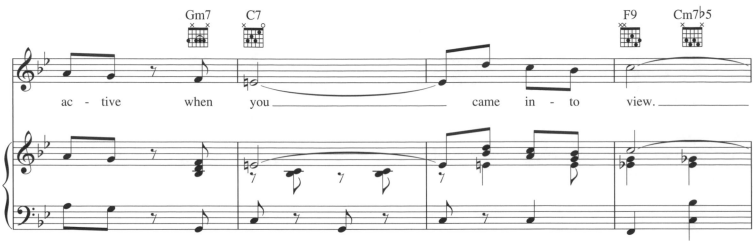

ac - tive when you _____ came in - to view. _____

___ I've got a crush on you, ___ Sweet - ie Pie. ___
crush on you, ___ Sweet - ie Pie. ___

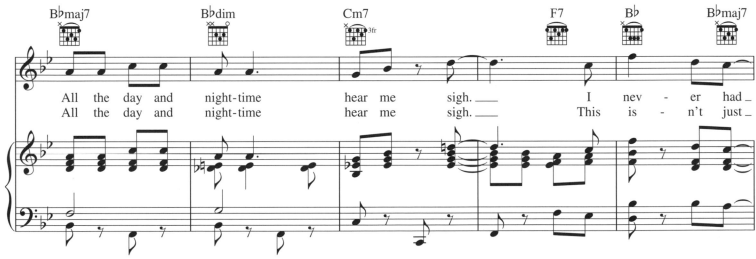

All the day and night-time hear me sigh. ___ I nev - er had __
All the day and night-time hear me sigh. ___ This is - n't just __

___ the least no - tion ___ that I could fall with ___ so much e -
___ a flir - ta - tion: ___ we're prov - ing that there's __ pre - des - ti -

CHEEK TO CHEEK
from the RKO Radio Motion Picture TOP HAT

Words and Music by
IRVING BERLIN

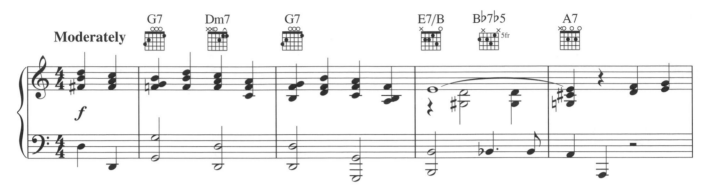

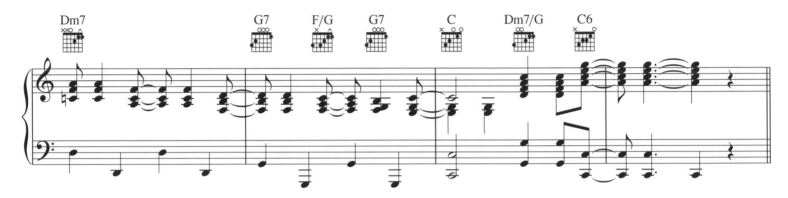

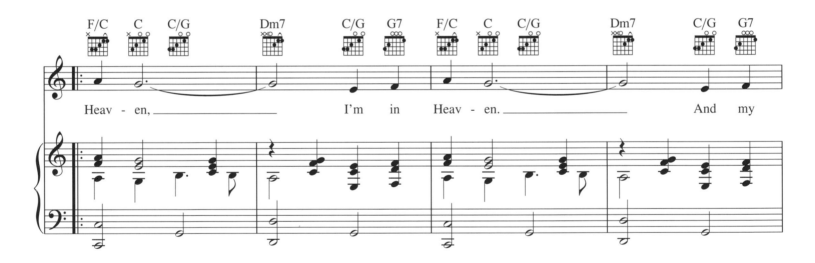

Heav - en, _____ I'm in Heav - en. _____ And my

heart beats so that I can hard - ly speak. _____ And I

39

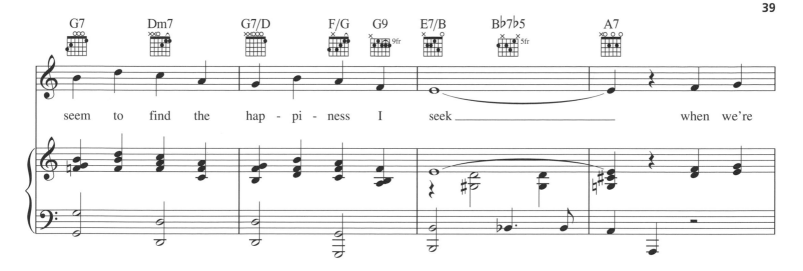

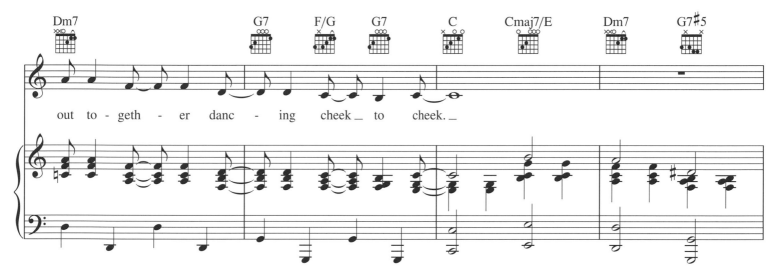

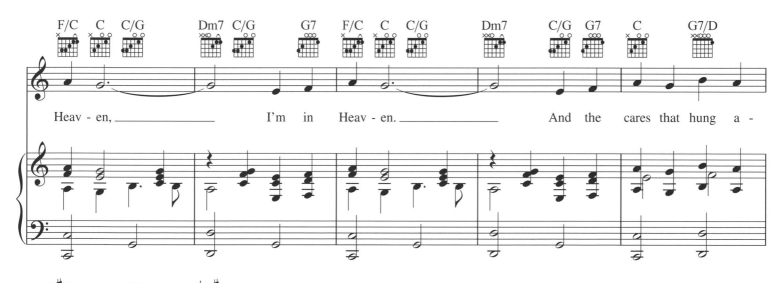

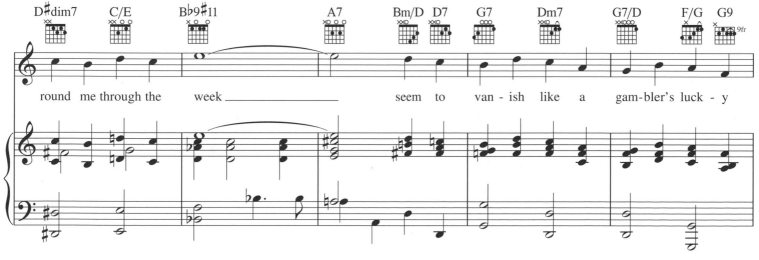

streak _____ when we're out to-geth - er danc - ing cheek to cheek.

_____ Oh, I love to climb a moun - tain, and to

reach the high-est peak, ___ but it does - n't thrill me half as much ___ as

danc - ing cheek to cheek. ___ Oh, I love to go out fish - ing in a

river or a creek, ___ but I don't en-joy it half as much as

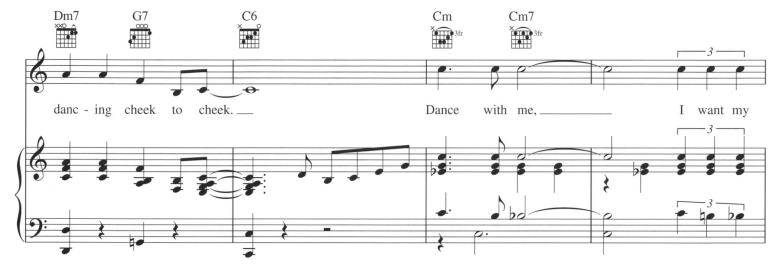

danc-ing cheek to cheek. ___ Dance with me, _____ I want my

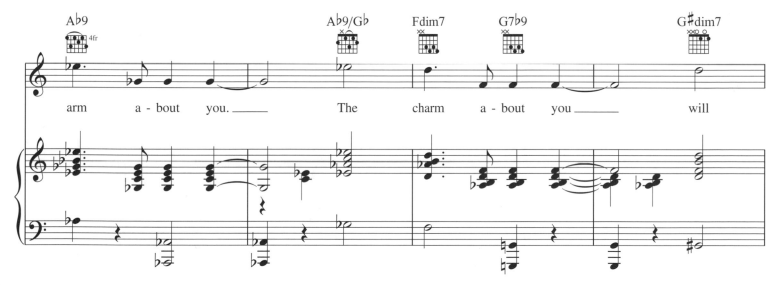

arm a-bout you. ___ The charm a-bout you _____ will

car-ry me through ___ to Heav-en, _____ I'm in

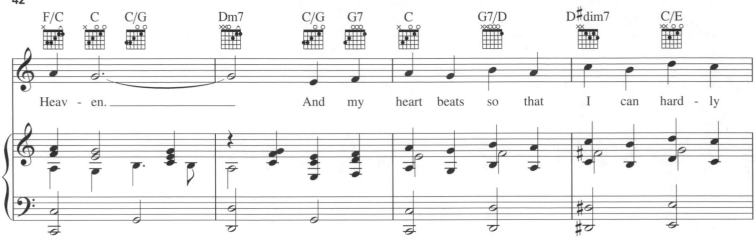

Heav - en. _____ And my heart beats so that I can hard - ly

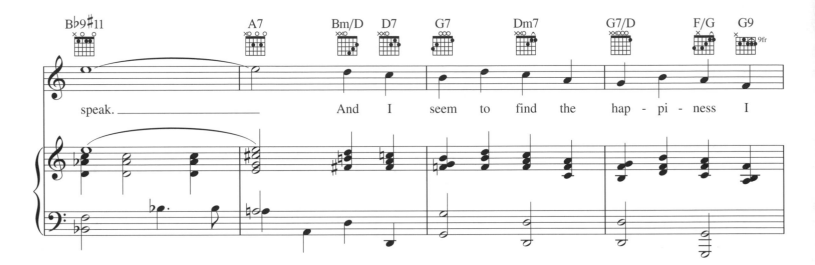

speak. _____ And I seem to find the hap - pi - ness I

seek _____ when we're out to - geth - er danc - ing cheek_ to cheek. _

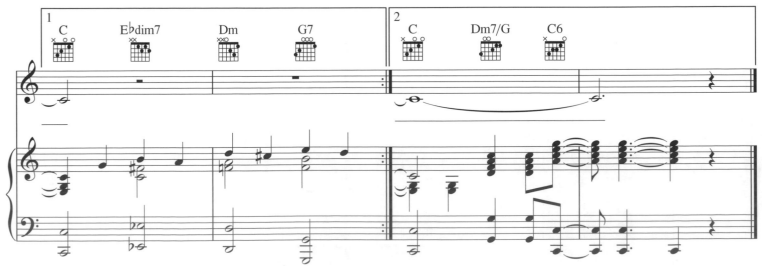

TRY A LITTLE TENDERNESS

Words and Music by HARRY WOODS,
JIMMY CAMPBELL and REG CONNELLY

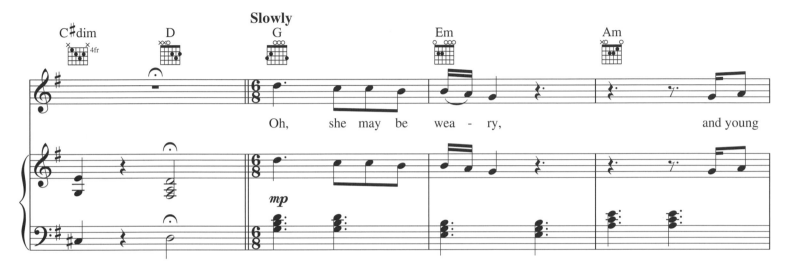

Oh, she may be wea - ry, and young

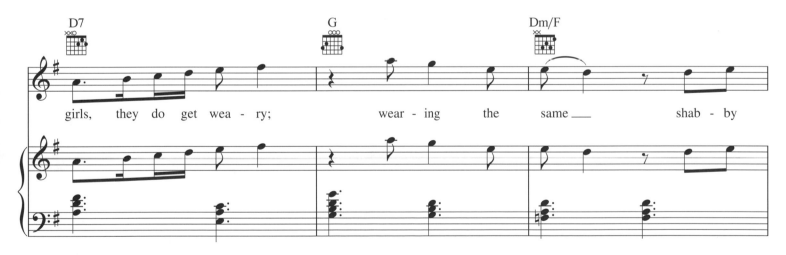

girls, they do get wea - ry; wear - ing the same ___ shab - by

dress. But

44

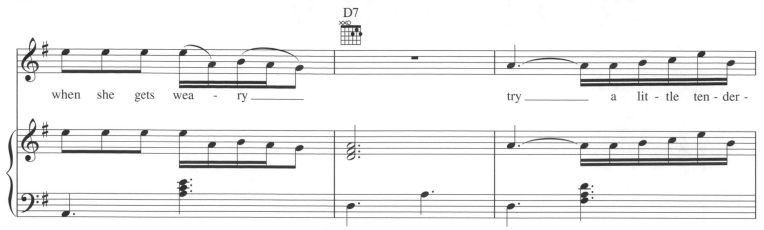

when she gets wea - ry _____ try _____ a lit - tle ten - der-

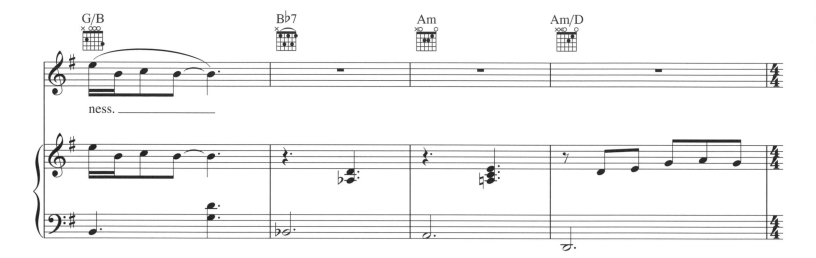

ness. _____

Moderately

You know she's wait - ing, _____ just an -
You won't re - gret it; _____ young girls,

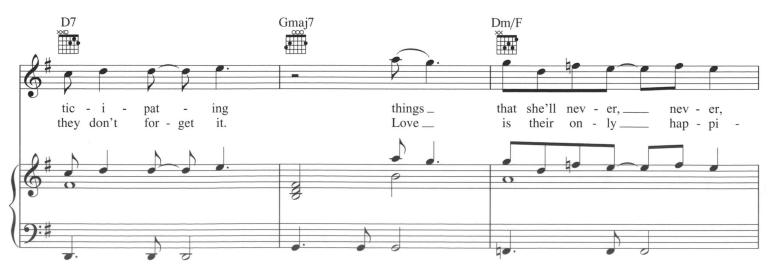

tic - i - pat - ing things _ that she'll nev - er, _____ nev - er,
they don't for - get it. Love _ is their on - ly _____ hap - pi -

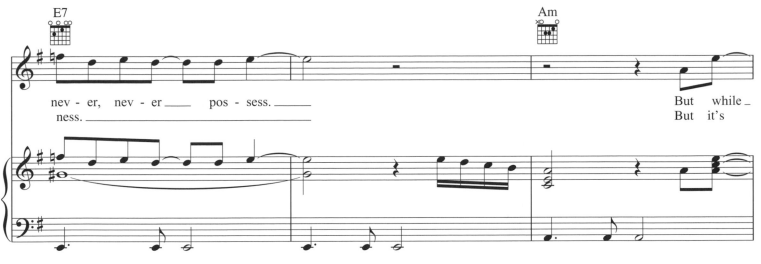

never, never ___ pos - sess. ___
ness. ___

But while ___
But it's

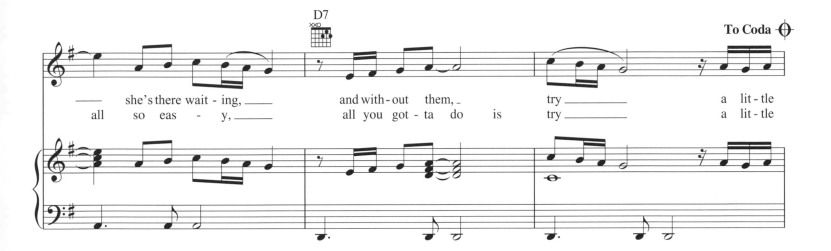

To Coda

___ she's there wait - ing, ___
all so eas - y, ___

and with-out them, ___
all you got - ta do is

try ___
try ___

a lit - tle
a lit - tle

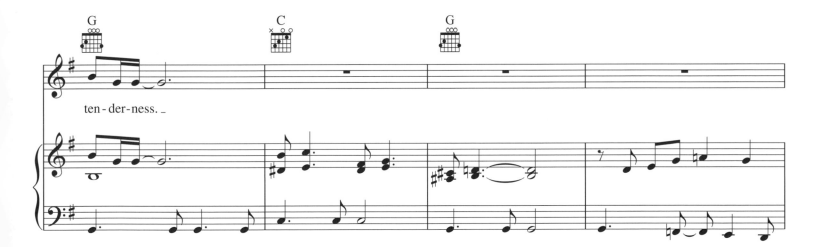

ten - der-ness. ___

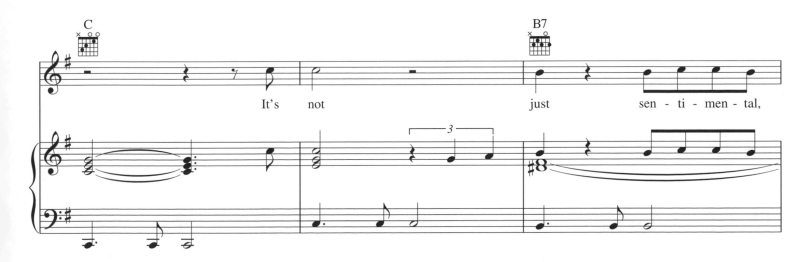

It's not

just

sen - ti - men - tal,

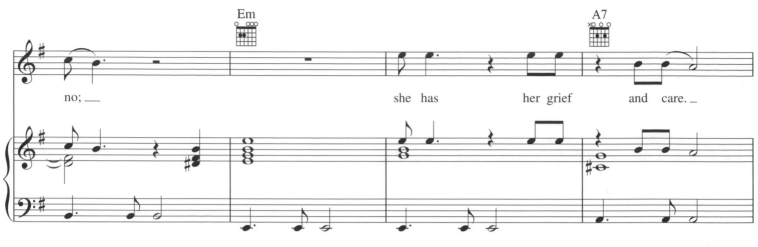

no; __ she has her grief and care. __

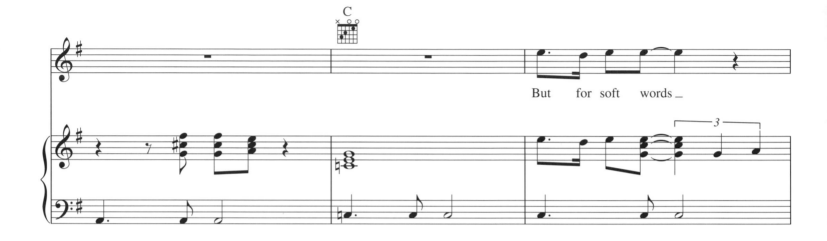

But for soft words __

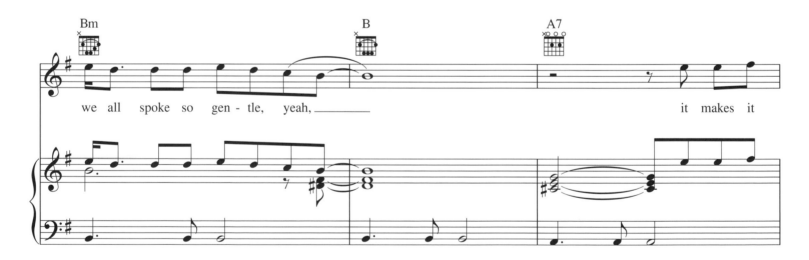

we all spoke so gen - tle, yeah, _____ it makes it

D.S. al Coda

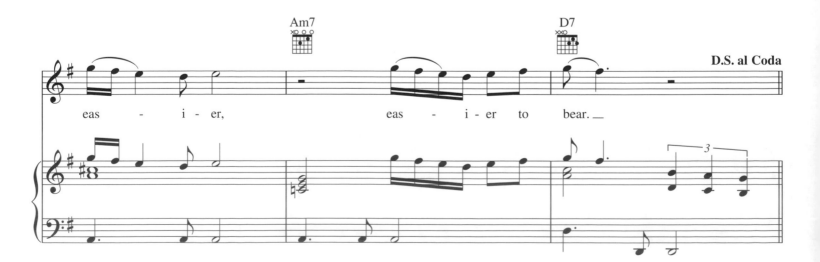

eas - i - er, eas - i - er to bear. __

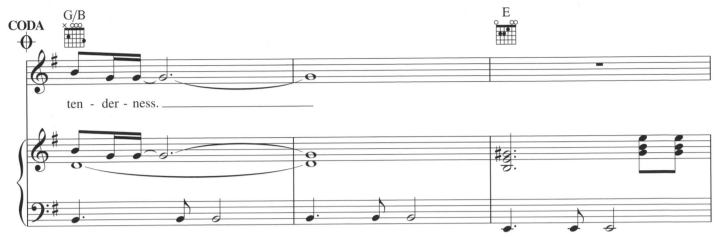

ten - der - ness._____

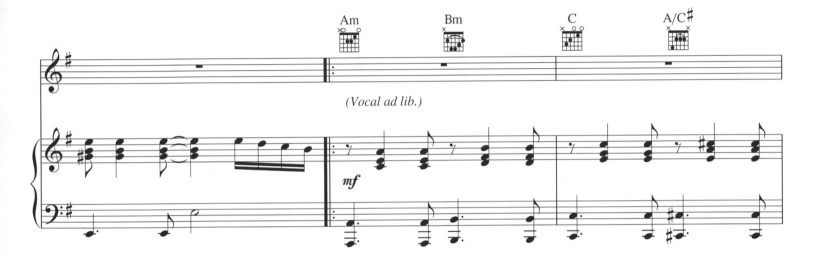

(Vocal ad lib.)

mf

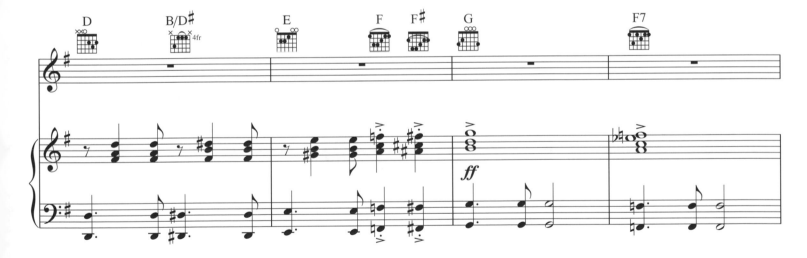

ff

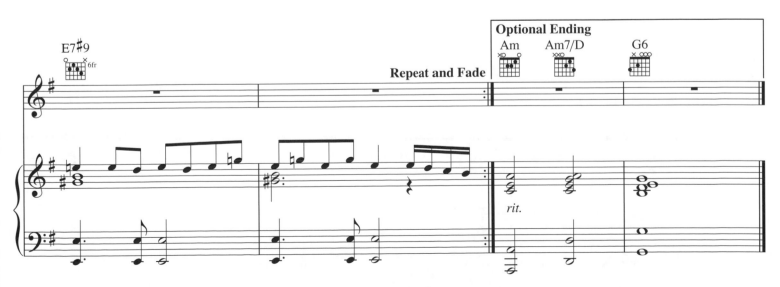

Optional Ending

Repeat and Fade

rit.

I WISH I WERE IN LOVE AGAIN

from BABES IN ARMS

Words by LORENZ HART
Music by RICHARD RODGERS

Moderately

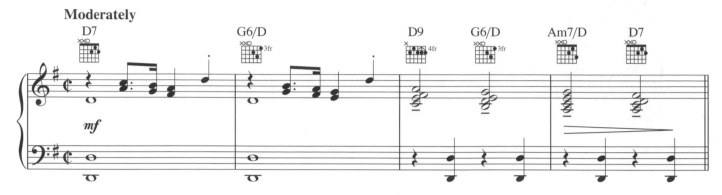

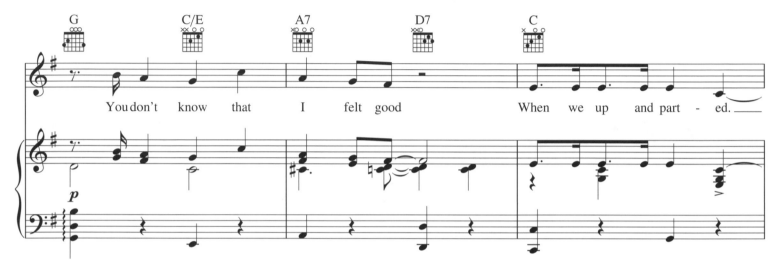

You don't know that I felt good When we up and part - ed. ___

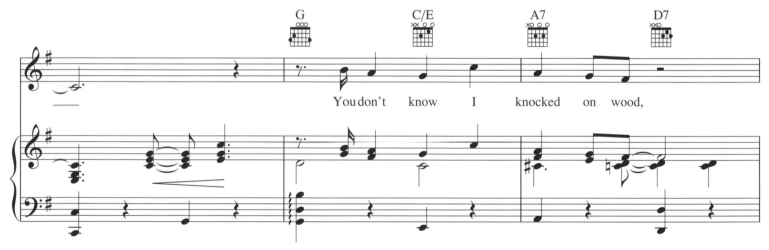

You don't know I knocked on wood,

Glad - ly bro - ken-heart - ed. ___ Wor - ry-ing is through, I

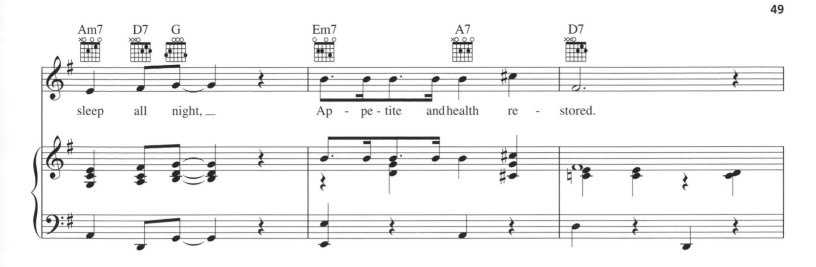

sleep all night, ___ Ap - pe - tite and health re - stored.

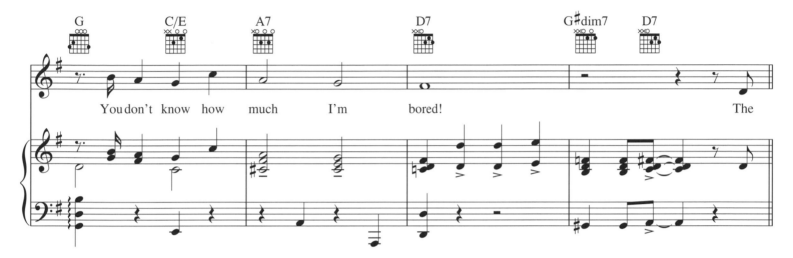

You don't know how much I'm bored! The

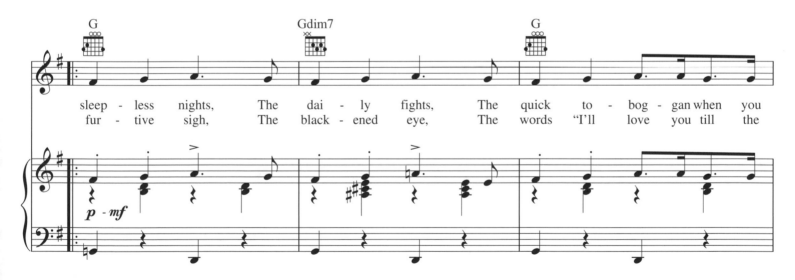

sleep - less nights, The dai - ly fights, The quick to - bog - gan when you
fur - tive sigh, The black - ened eye, The words "I'll love you till the

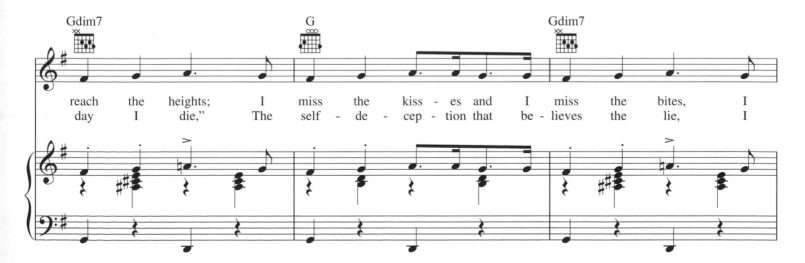

reach the heights; I miss the kiss - es and I miss the bites, I
day I die," The self - de - cep - tion that be - lieves the lie, I

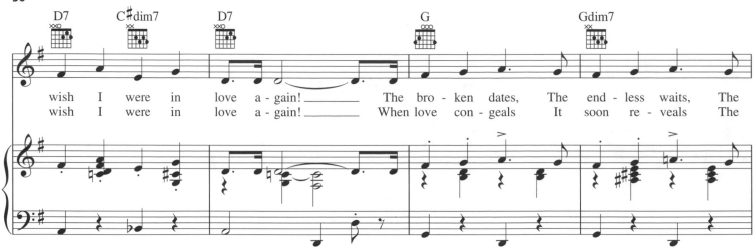

wish I were in love a - gain! _____ The bro - ken dates, The end - less waits, The
wish I were in love a - gain! _____ When love con - geals It soon re - veals The

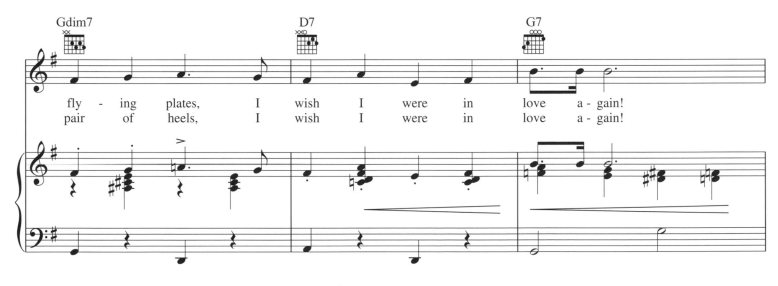

love - ly lov - ing and the hate - ful hates, The con - ver - sa - tion with the
faint a - ro - ma of per - form - ing seals, The dou - ble - cross - ing of a

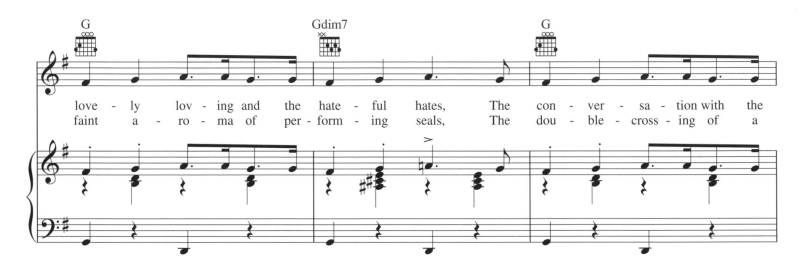

fly - ing plates, I wish I were in love a - gain!
pair of heels, I wish I were in love a - gain!

No ____ more pain, No ____ more strain,
No ____ more care, No ____ de - spair.

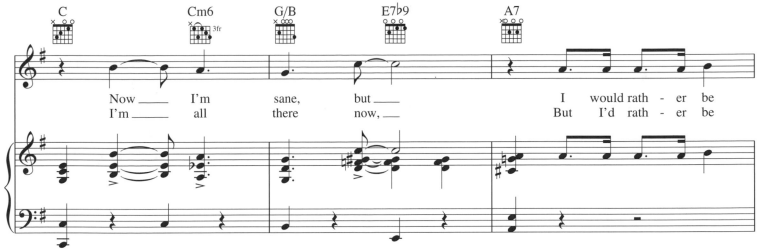

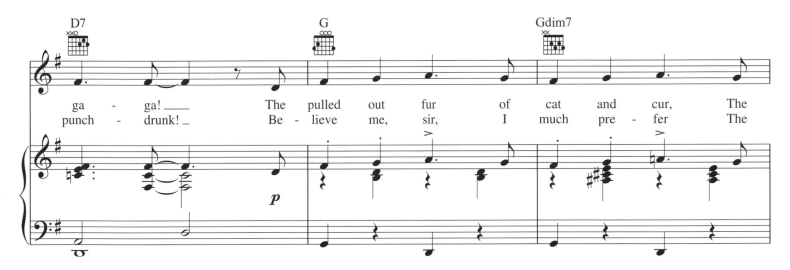

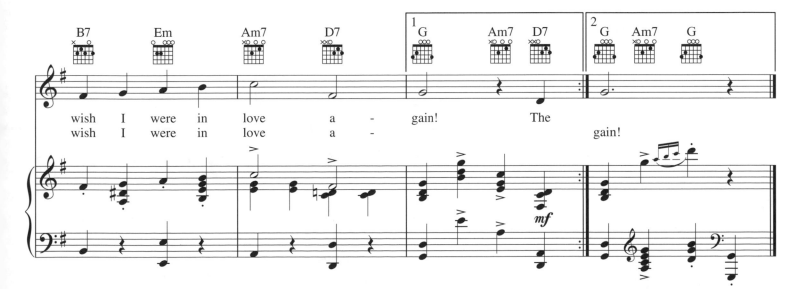

ANGEL EYES

Words by EARL BRENT
Music by MATT DENNIS

Moderately slow

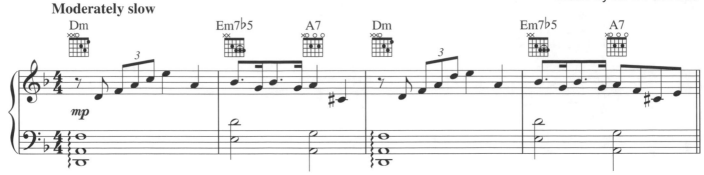

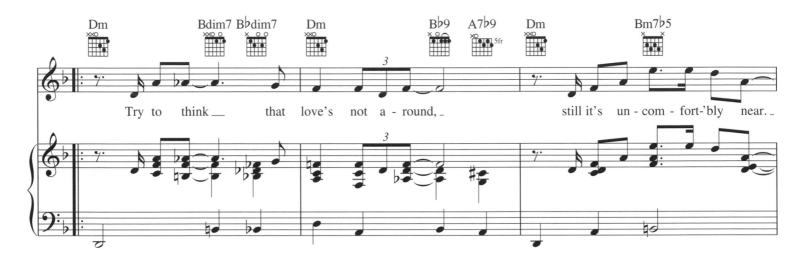

Try to think ___ that love's not a-round, ___ still it's un-com-fort-'bly near. ___

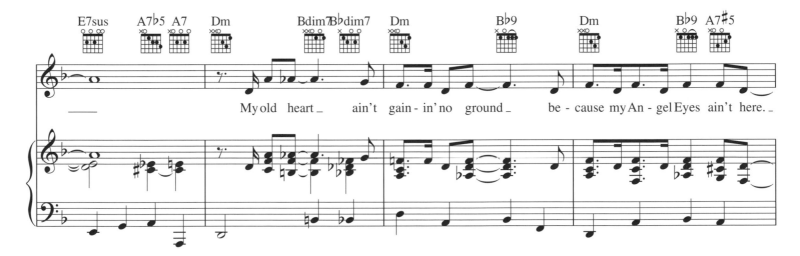

___ My old heart ___ ain't gain-in' no ground ___ be-cause my An-gel Eyes ain't here. ___

___ An-gel Eyes ___ that old dev-il sent, ___

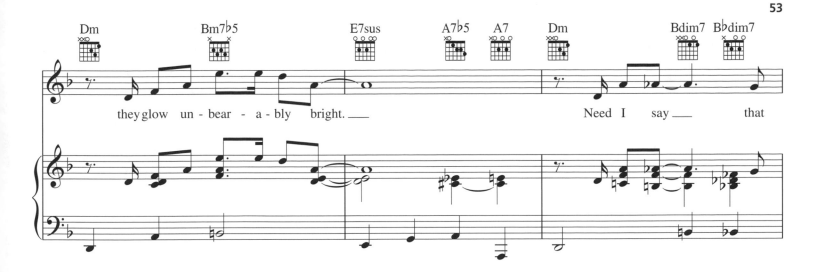

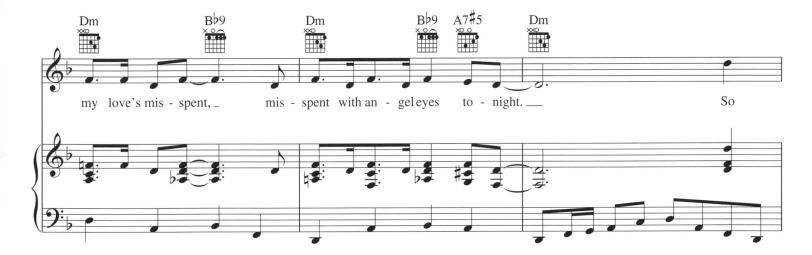

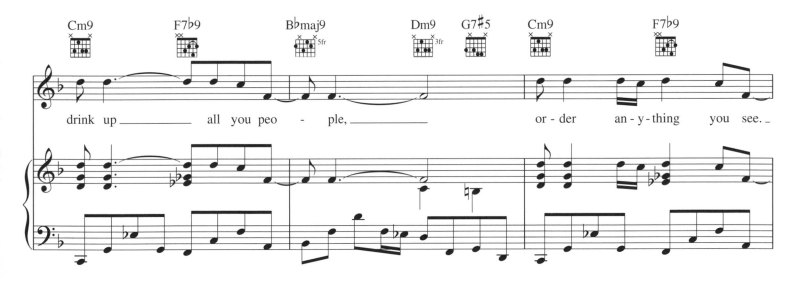

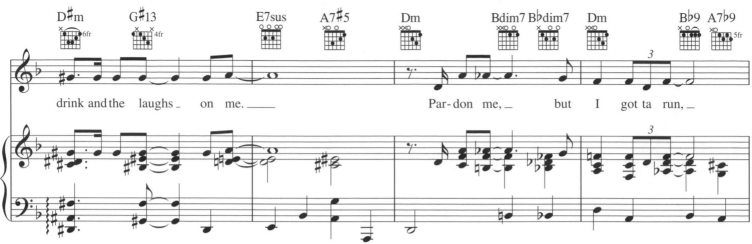

drink and the laughs ___ on me. ___ Par-don me, ___ but I got ta run, ___

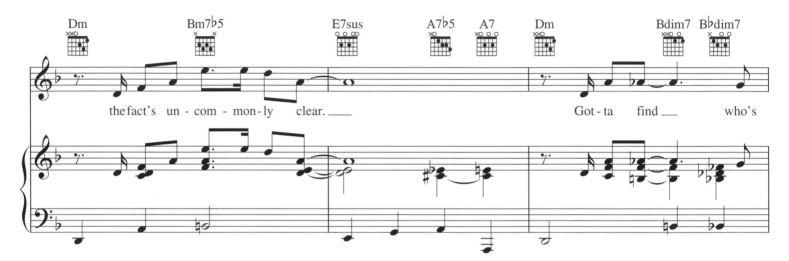

the fact's un - com - mon - ly clear. ___ Got - ta find ___ who's

now "Num-ber One" ___ and why my An - gel Eyes ain't here. ___

'Scuse me while I dis - ap - pear. ___

IN THE WEE SMALL HOURS
OF THE MORNING

Words by BOB HILLIARD
Music by DAVID MANN

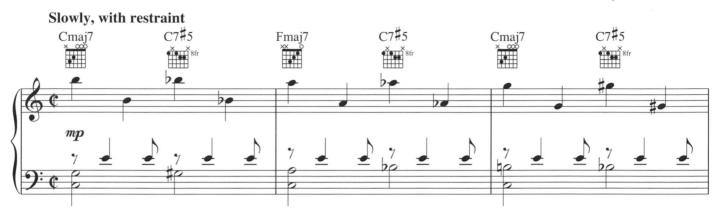

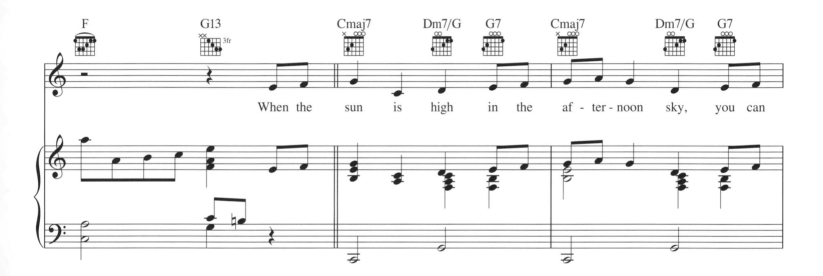

When the sun is high in the af-ter-noon sky, you can

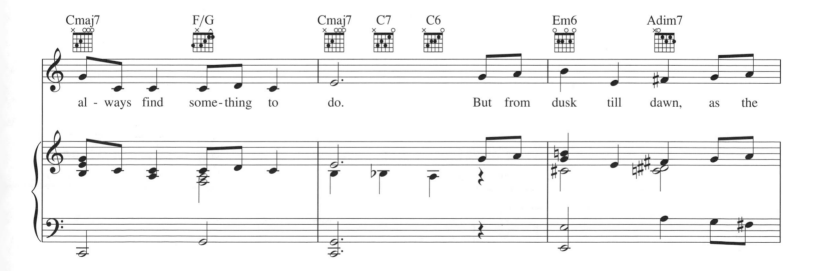

al-ways find some-thing to do. But from dusk till dawn, as the

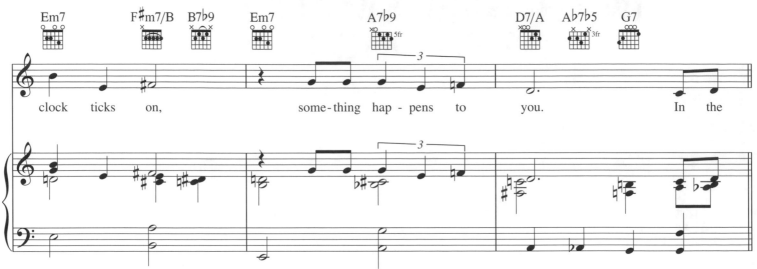

clock ticks on, some-thing hap-pens to you. In the

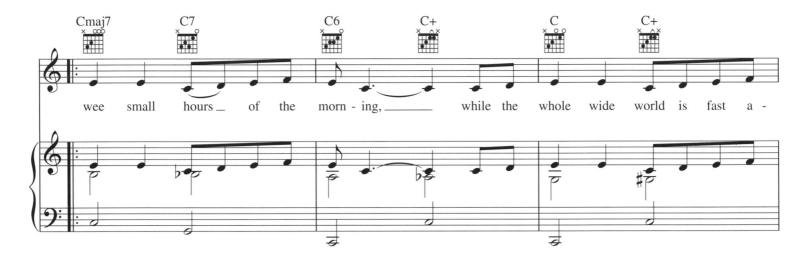

wee small hours _ of the morn - ing, _____ while the whole wide world is fast a -

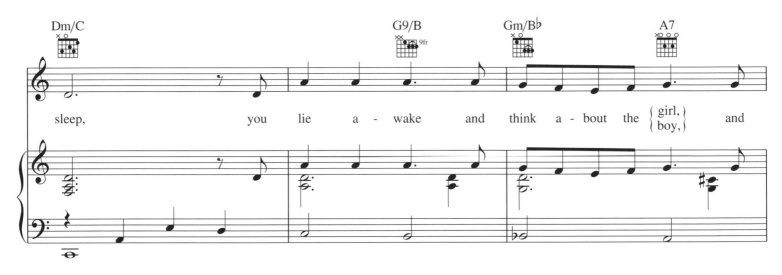

sleep, you lie a - wake and think a - bout the { girl, } { boy, } and

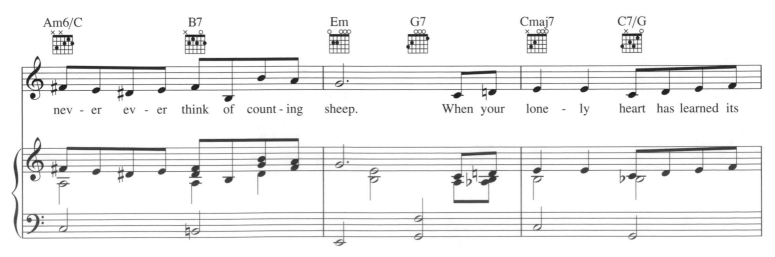

nev - er ev - er think of count - ing sheep. When your lone - ly heart has learned its

AS TIME GOES BY

from CASABLANCA

Words and Music by
HERMAN HUPFELD

Moderately

This day and age we're liv-ing in gives cause for ap-pre-hen-sion, With

speed and new in-ven-tion, and things like third di-men-sion, Yet we get a tri-fle wea-ry, with

Mis-ter Ein-stein's the-'ry, so we must get down to earth, at times re-lax, re-lieve the ten-sion. No

AT LONG LAST LOVE

from YOU NEVER KNOW

Words and Music by
COLE PORTER

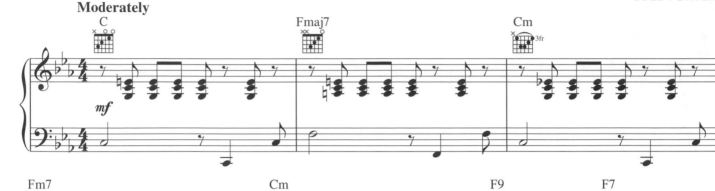

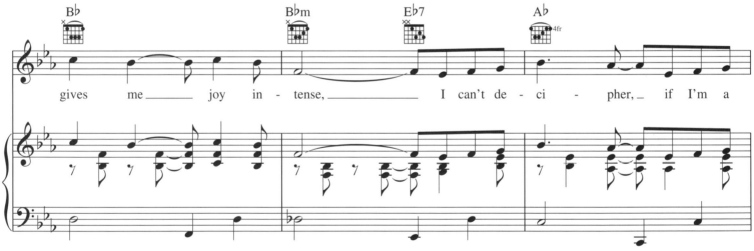

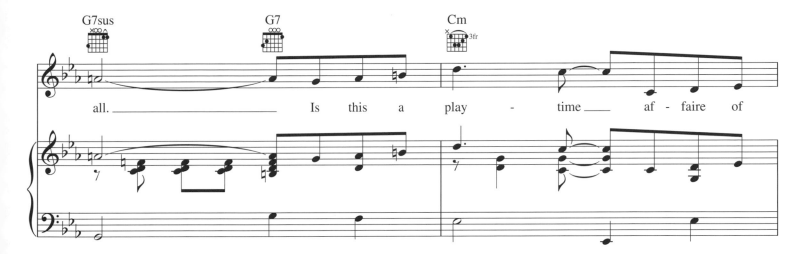

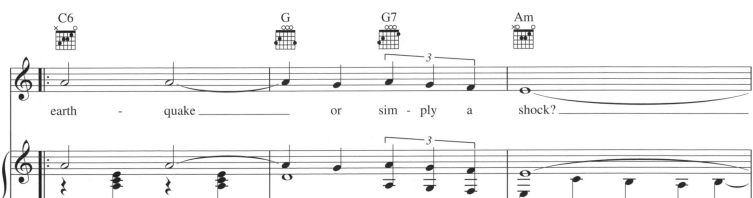

Is it the good tur - tle soup or mere - ly the

mock? _____ Is it a cock - tail, _____ this feel - ing of

joy, _____ or is what I feel the real Mc -

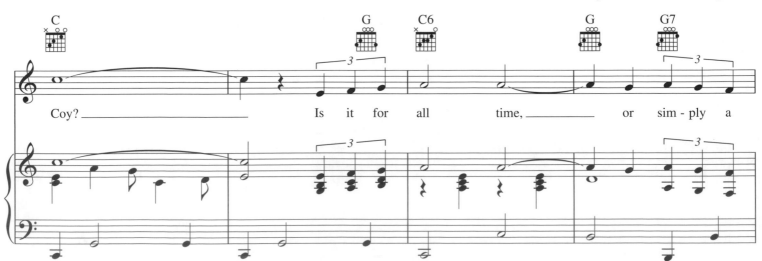

Coy? _____ Is it for all time, _____ or sim - ply a

65

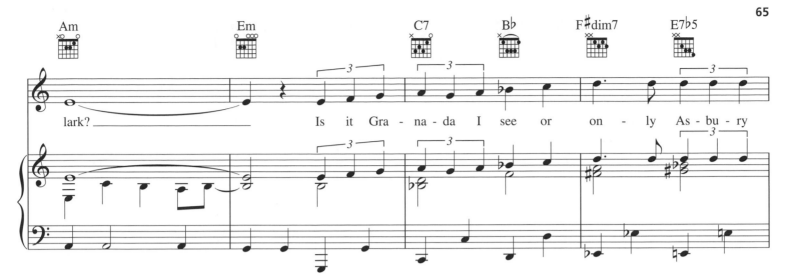

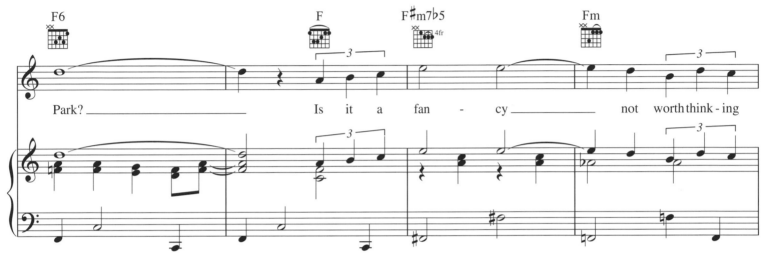

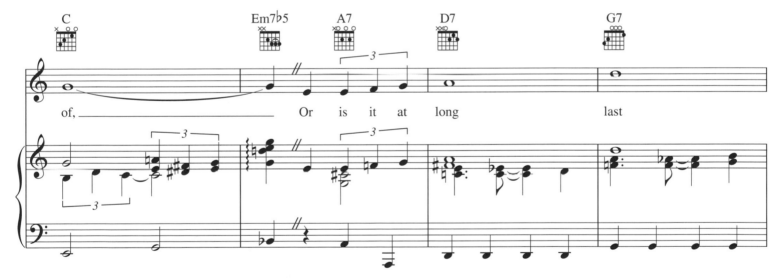

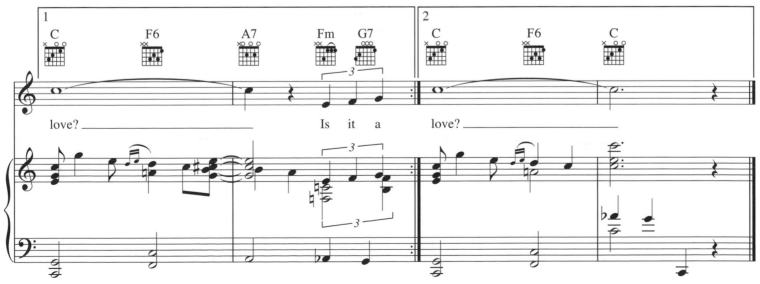

I'LL BE SEEING YOU

from RIGHT THIS WAY

Lyric by IRVING KAHAL
Music by SAMMY FAIN

Moderately

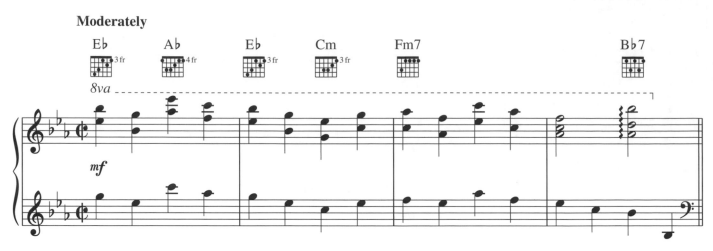

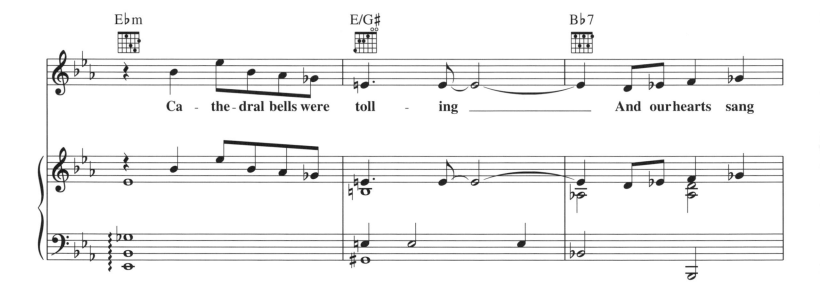

Ca - the-dral bells were toll - ing _____ And our hearts sang

on, _____ Was it the spell of Par - is _____

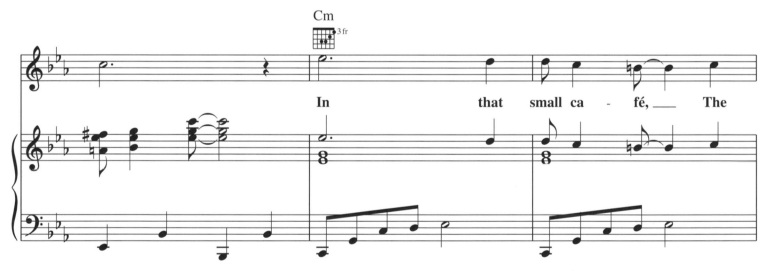

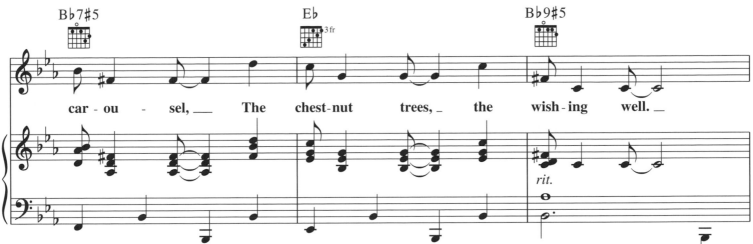

car - ou - sel, ___ The chest-nut trees, _ the wish - ing well. _

I'll be see - ing you ___ In ev - 'ry love - ly

sum - mer's day, In ev - 'ry-thing that's light and gay, I'll

al - ways think of you that way. I'll find you in the

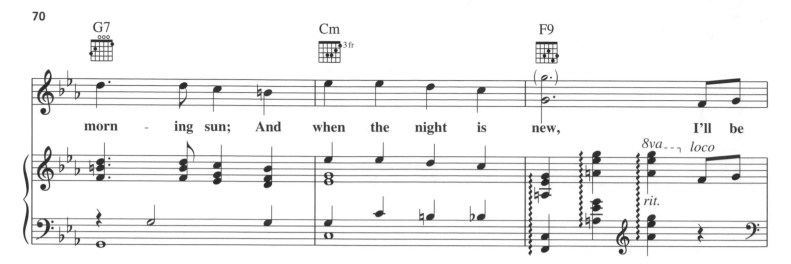

morn - ing sun; And when the night is new, I'll be

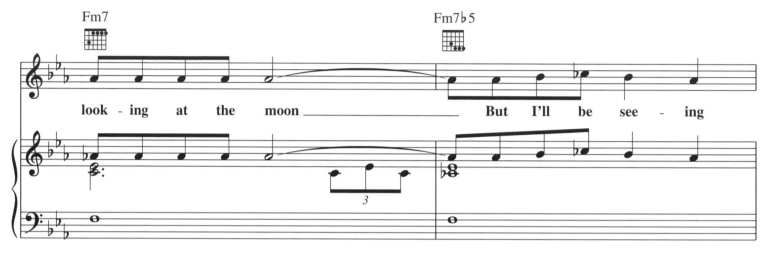

look - ing at the moon _____ But I'll be see - ing

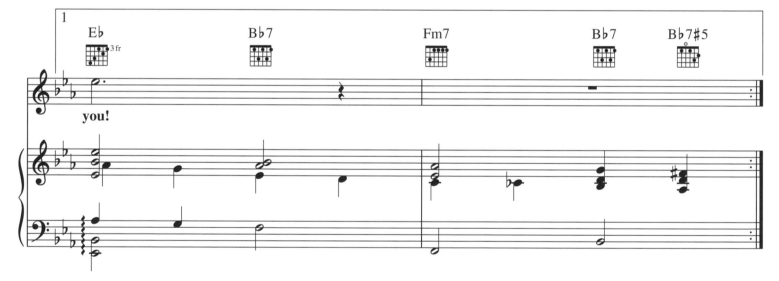

you!

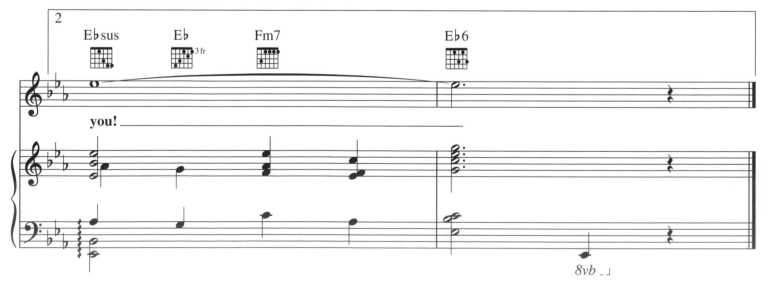

you! _____

ALMOST LIKE BEING IN LOVE
from BRIGADOON

Lyrics by ALAN JAY LERNER
Music by FREDERICK LOEWE

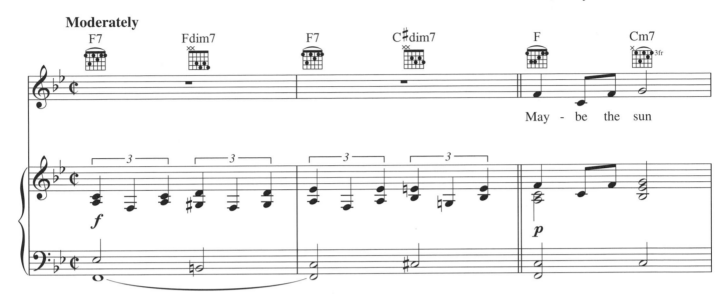

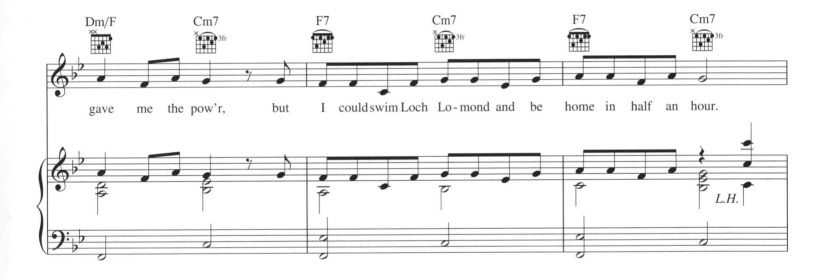

72

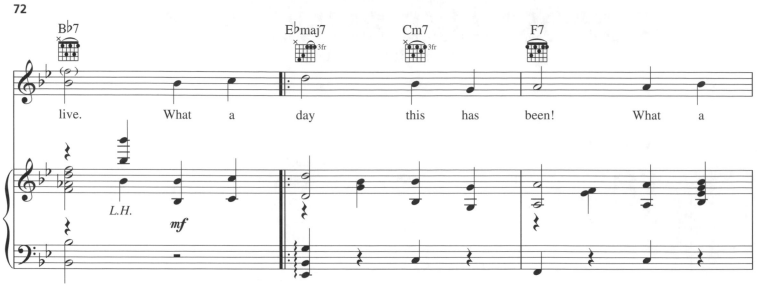

live. What a day this has been! What a

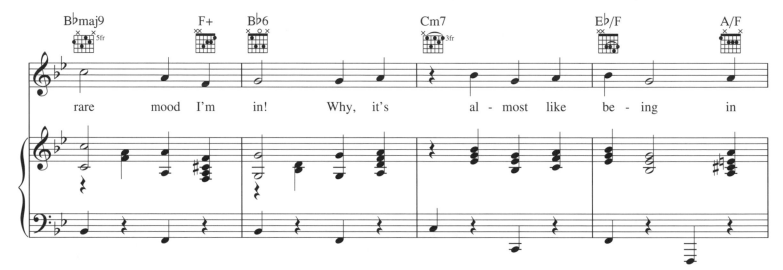

rare mood I'm in! Why, it's al-most like be-ing in

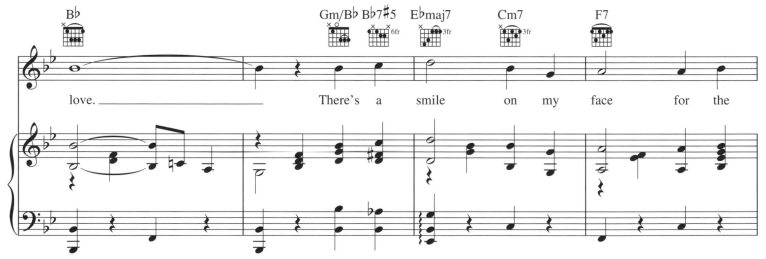

love. _____ There's a smile on my face for the

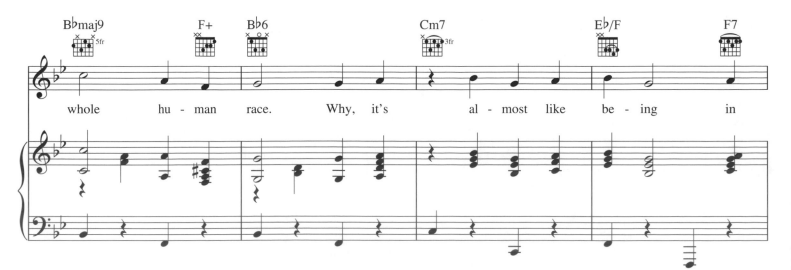

whole hu-man race. Why, it's al-most like be-ing in

love! _____ All the mu - sic of

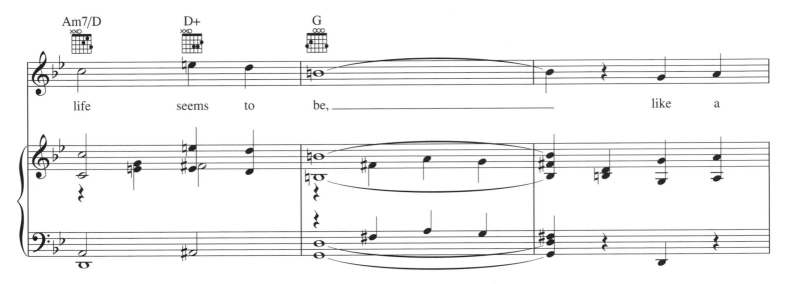

life seems to be, _____ like a

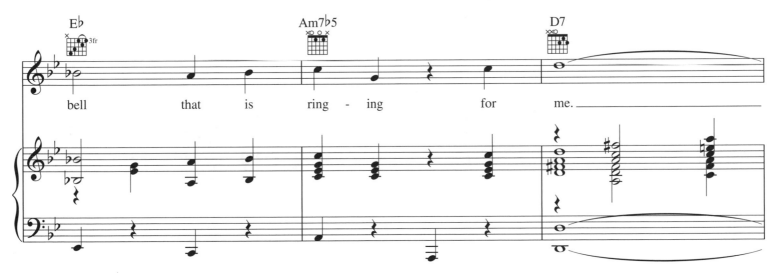

bell that is ring - ing for me. _____

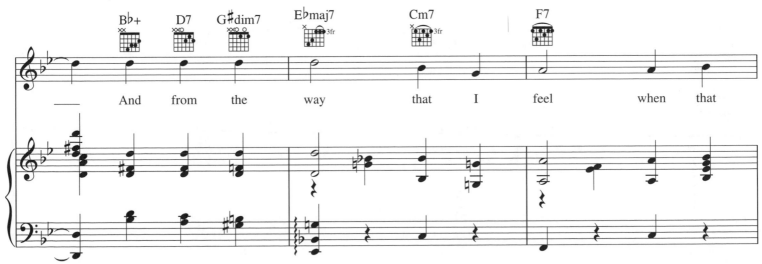

___ And from the way that I feel when that

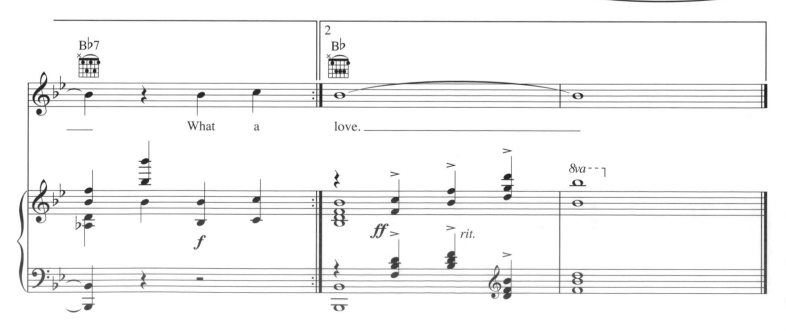

EMBRACEABLE YOU

from CRAZY FOR YOU

Music and Lyrics by GEORGE GERSHWIN
and IRA GERSHWIN

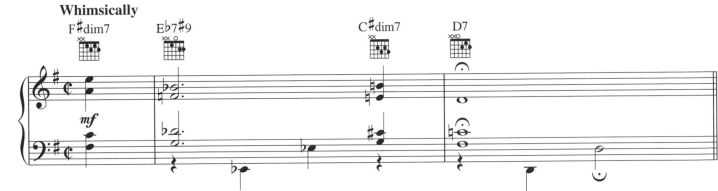

Doz - ens of girls would storm ___ up; I had to lock my

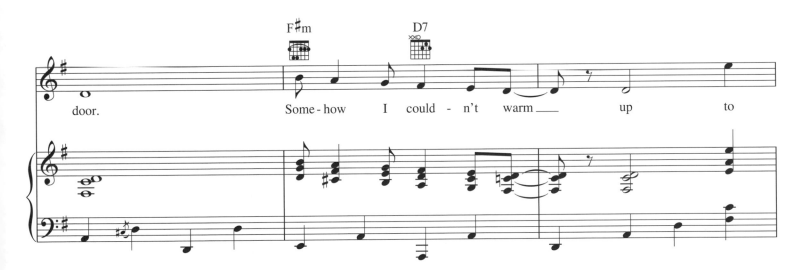

door. Some - how I could - n't warm ___ up to

one be - fore. What was it that con - trolled ___ me?

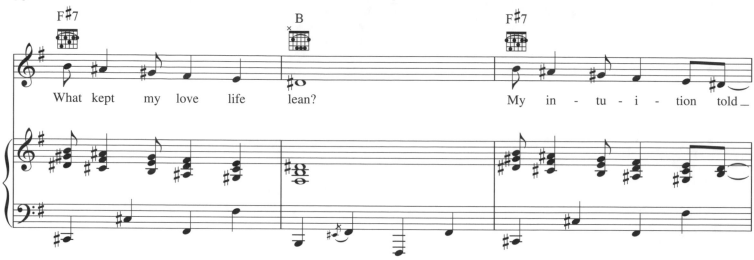

What kept my love life lean? My in - tu - i - tion told _

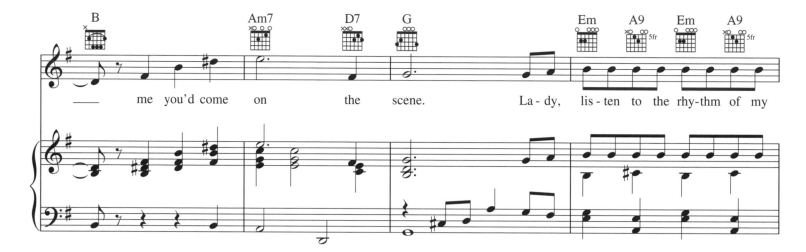

_ me you'd come on the scene. La - dy, lis - ten to the rhy-thm of my

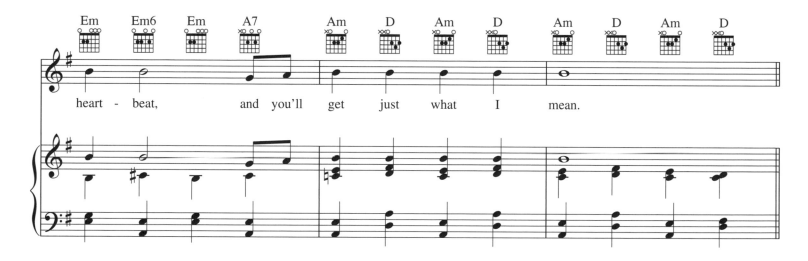

heart - beat, and you'll get just what I mean.

Em - brace me, my sweet em - brace - a - ble you! _

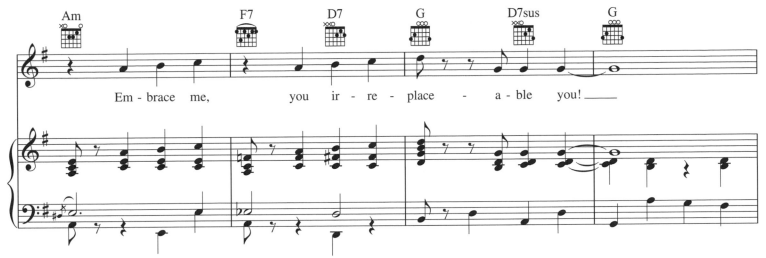

Em-brace me, you ir-re-place - a-ble you! _____

Just one look at you, my heart grew tip - sy in me; _____

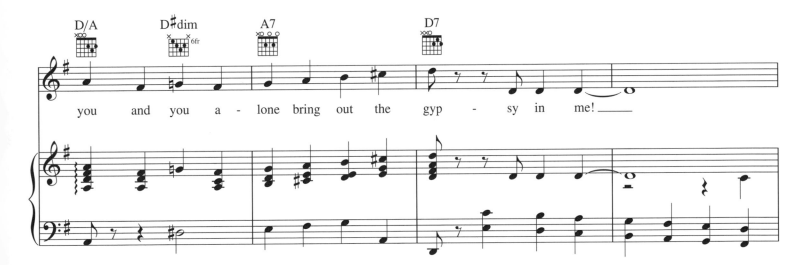

you and you a - lone bring out the gyp - sy in me! _____

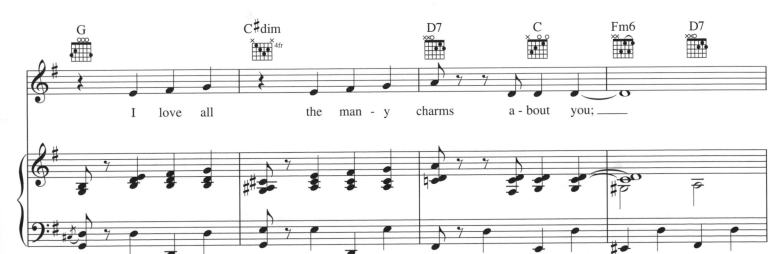

I love all the man - y charms a-bout you; _____

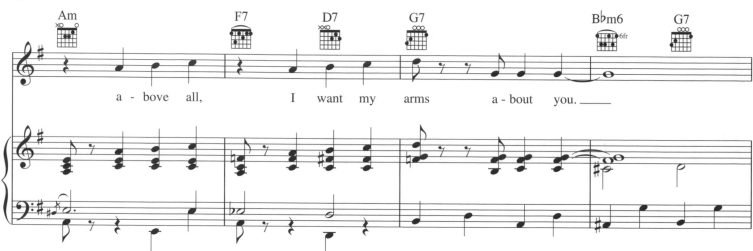

a - bove all, I want my arms a - bout you. _____

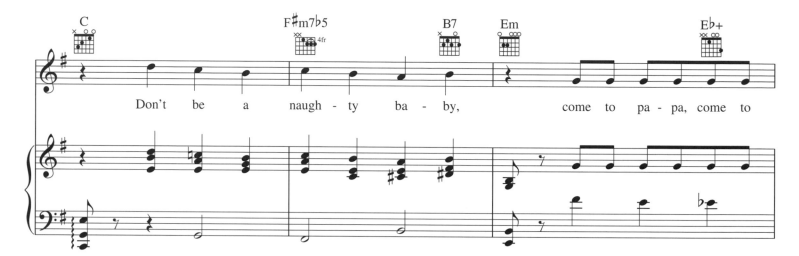

Don't be a naugh - ty ba - by, come to pa - pa, come to

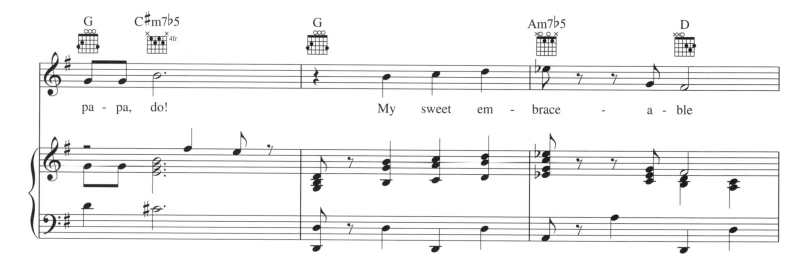

pa - pa, do! My sweet em - brace - a - ble

you! you! _____

NICE 'N' EASY

Words and Music by LEW SPENCE,
ALAN BERGMAN and MARILYN BERGMAN

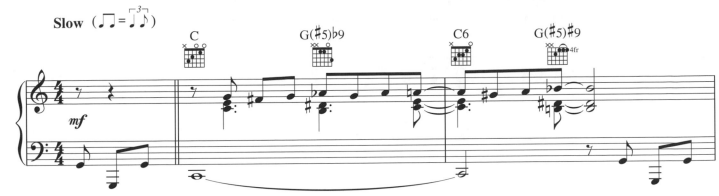

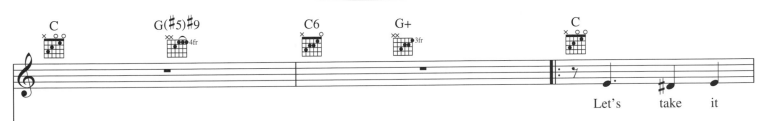

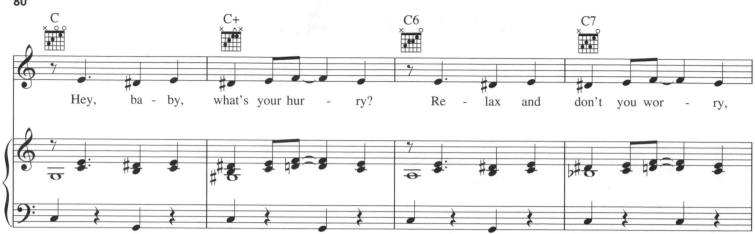

Hey, ba - by, what's your hur - ry? Re - lax and don't you wor - ry,

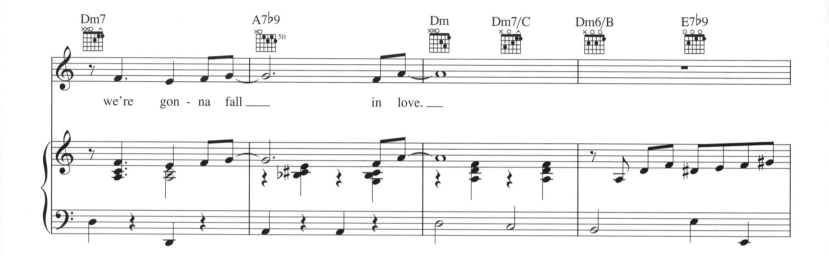

we're gon - na fall ____ in love. ____

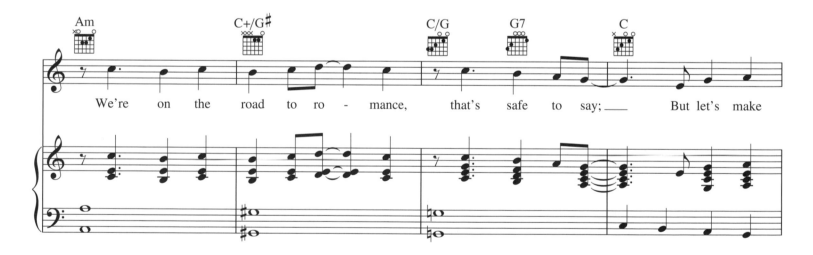

We're on the road to ro - mance, that's safe to say; ____ But let's make

all the stops ____ a - long ____ the way. ____

The prob-lem now, of course, _ is to sim - ply hold your hors - es,

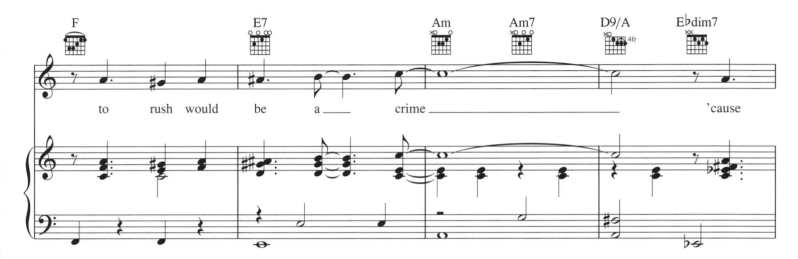

to rush would be a ____ crime _____ 'cause

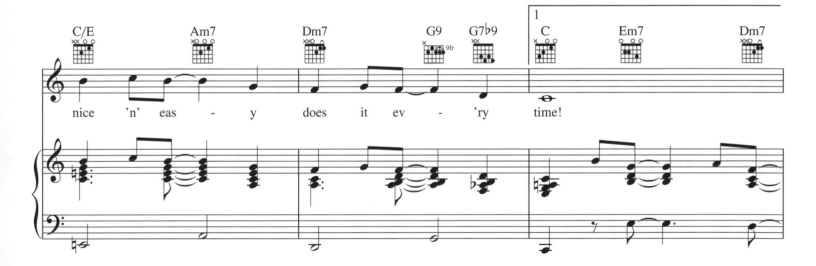

nice 'n' eas - y does it ev - 'ry time!

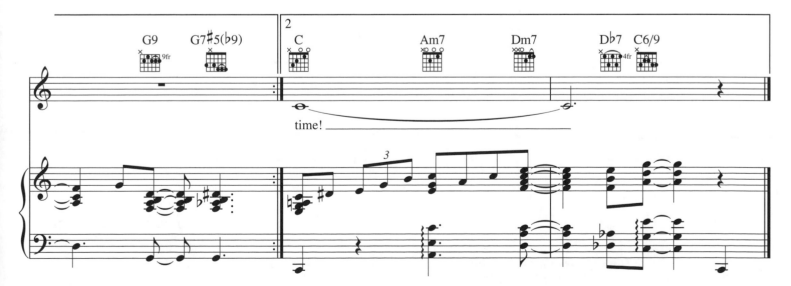

time! ____

WHERE OR WHEN

from BABES IN ARMS

Words by LORENZ HART
Music by RICHARD RODGERS

When you're a-wake, the things you think come from the dreams you dream.

Thought has wings, _____ and lots of things _____ are sel-dom what they seem.

Some-times you think you've lived be - fore all that you live to - day.

Things you do _____ come back to you, _____ as though they knew the way. Oh, the

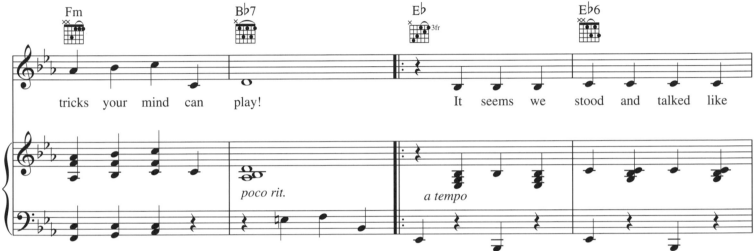

tricks your mind can play! It seems we stood and talked like

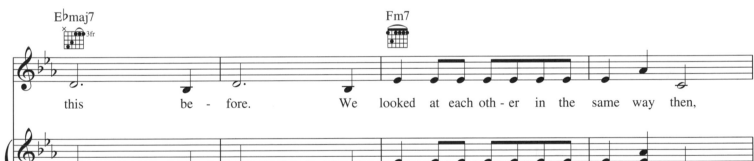

this be - fore. We looked at each oth - er in the same way then,

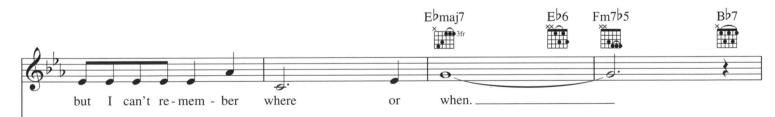

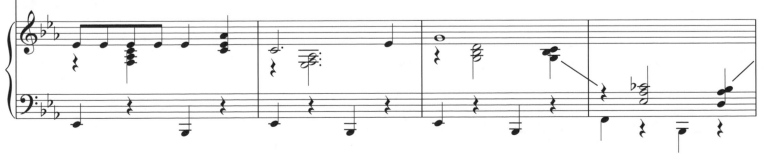

but I can't re-mem - ber where or when. _____

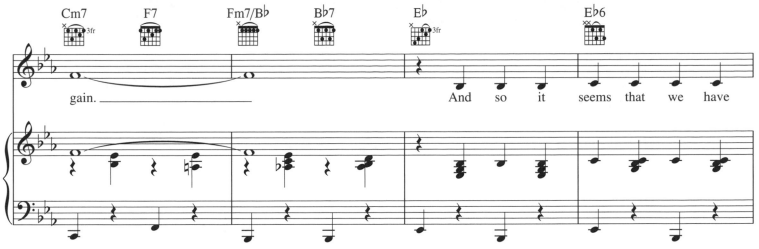

gain. _____ And so it seems that we have

met be - fore, and laughed be - fore, and

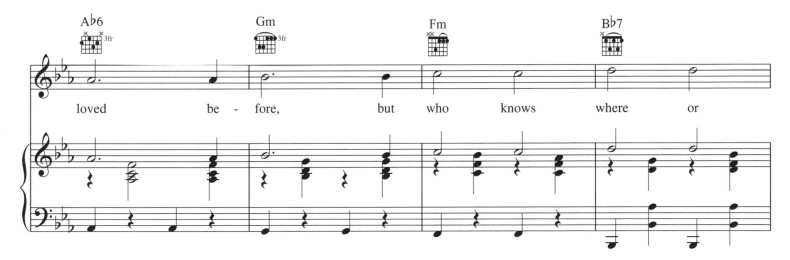

loved be - fore, but who knows where or

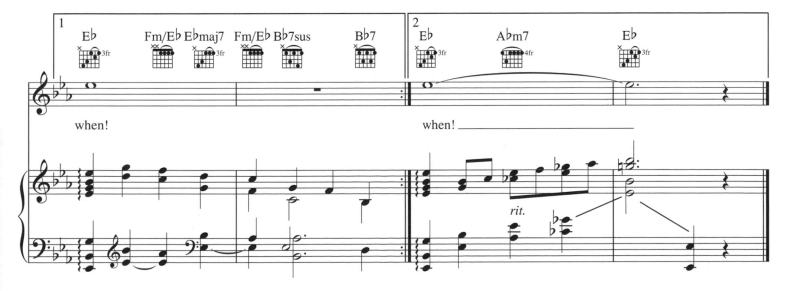

when! when! _____

IF YOU ARE BUT A DREAM

Words and Music by NATHAN BONX,
JACK FULTON and MOE JAFFE

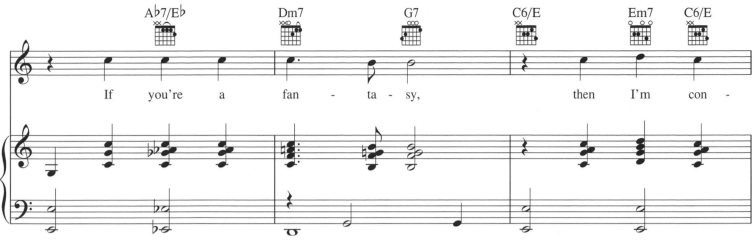

If you're a fan - ta - sy, then I'm con -

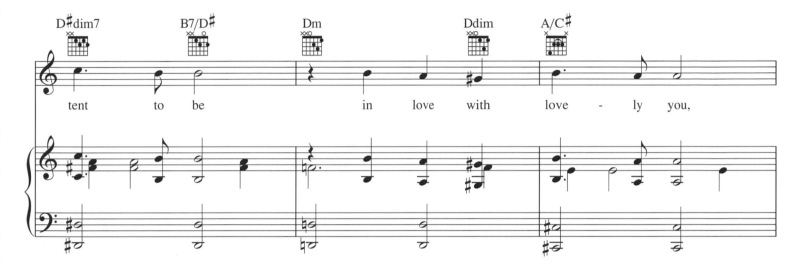

tent to be in love with love - ly you,

and pray my dream comes true. I long to

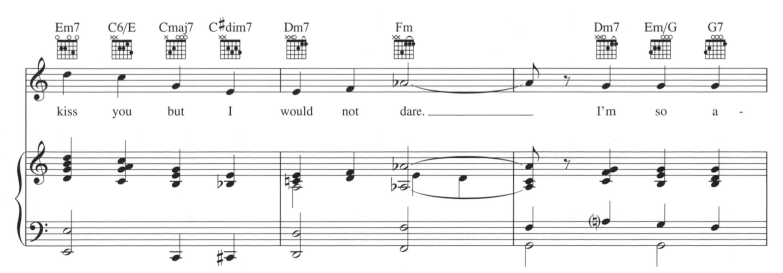

kiss you but I would not dare. _____ I'm so a -

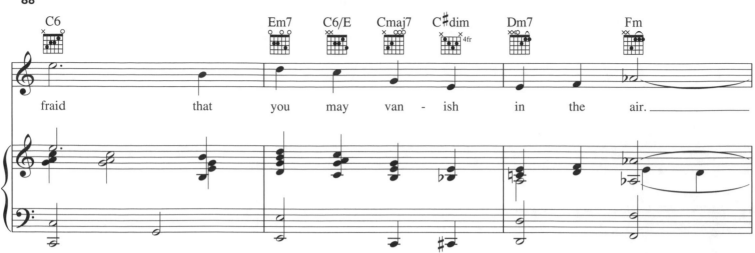

fraid   that   you   may   van - ish   in   the   air. _____

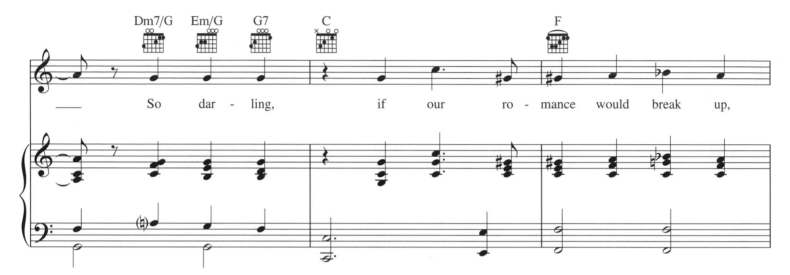

_____ So   dar - ling,   if   our   ro - mance   would   break   up,

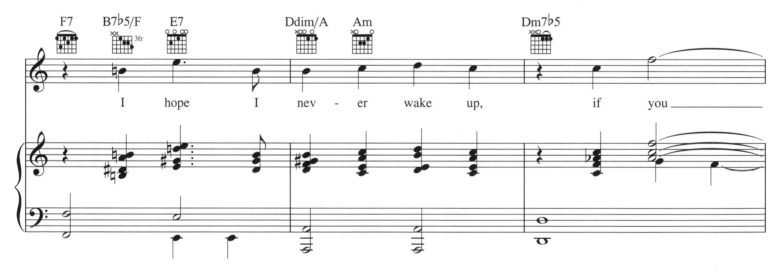

I   hope   I   nev - er   wake   up,   if   you _____

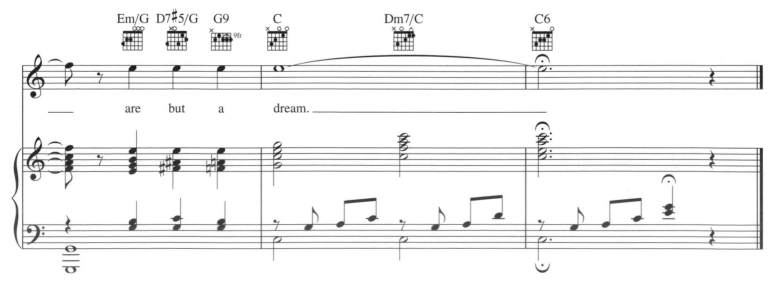

_____ are   but   a   dream. _____